Always Being Reformed

Also from Westminster John Knox Press
by Shirley C. Guthrie

Christian Doctrine, revised edition
Diversity in Faith—Unity in Christ

Always Being Reformed

Faith for a Fragmented World

SHIRLEY C. GUTHRIE

Westminster John Knox Press
Louisville, Kentucky

© 1996 Shirley C. Guthrie

Scripture quotations from the New Revised Standard Version of the Bible are copyright © 1989 by the Division of Christian Education of the National Council of the Churches of Christ in the U.S.A. and are used by permission.

The lecture that became the fourth chapter of this book was published in the April 1996 edition of *Theology Today.* The lecture that was revised to become the fifth chapter of this book was published in *The Princeton Seminary Bulletin,* vol. XVII, no. 1, new series, 1996. Both are reprinted here by permission.

Book design by Jennifer K. Cox
Cover design by Kim Wohlenhaus

First edition

Published by Westminster John Knox Press
Louisville, Kentucky

This book is printed on acid-free paper that meets the American National Standards Institute Z39.48 standard. ⊚

PRINTED IN THE UNITED STATES OF AMERICA

96 97 98 99 00 01 02 03 04 05 — 10 9 8 7 6 5 4 3 2 1

Library of Congress Cataloging-in-Publication Data

Guthrie, Shirley C., date.
    Always being reformed : the Reformed confessional tradition in a pluralistic world / Shirley C. Guthrie — 1st ed.
        p.   cm.
    Includes bibliographical references.
    ISBN 0-664-25683-X (alk. paper)
    1. Church. 2. Reformed Church—Doctrines. 3. Presbyterian Church —Doctrines. 4. Mission of the church. 5. Identification (Religion) 6. Religious pluralism—Christianity. 7. Reformed Church—Membership. 8. Presbyterian Church—Membership. I. Title.
BV600.2.G88   1996
284'.2—dc20   96-17777

For Allan and Janet
And in memory of our mother and father

Contents

Preface

The chapters in this book are a slightly expanded version of the Warfield Lectures delivered at Princeton Theological Seminary in the spring of 1995. I am grateful for the invitation of President Thomas Gillespie and the faculty to give the lectures and for the friendly and probing response they received from faculty members, students, and visitors on the campus. As I prepared and delivered the lectures I also remembered with gratitude my first teachers of theology, Paul Lehmann and George S. Hendry, who introduced me and many other Princeton students to the joyful freedom of "doing" theology in service of the promises and demands of a gracious triune God, and who set me on the way I have tried to follow as a theologian and teacher of theology.

I could not have written the lectures and this book without many conversations with my colleagues C. Benton Kline and George W. Stroup. They listened and read, questioned and corrected, encouraged and offered constructive suggestions—then, like the good teachers they are, helped me to say more clearly what I wanted to say even at points where they disagreed with me. I alone am responsible for errors in fact and interpretation that are still there.

I am grateful to acquisitions editor Timothy G. Staveteig, to copyediting manager Nancy J. Roseberry, and to copyeditor Esther Kolb at Westminster John Knox Press for their encouragement and insightful help in preparing the manuscript for publication. I am also grateful to my colleague and friend Ann Titshaw, who typed and retyped the manuscript with the same unfailing patience, cheerfulness, and support with which she has worked with and for me in the past.

A Tale of
Two Churches

As I began to write this book, I had two very different local churches in mind.

The first is a downtown church that has refused to flee to the suburbs but has stayed to minister at the same time to members of the political and business establishments of the city; to the poor, mostly black people who live in the inner city; and to others around town who have felt excluded or unhappy in other churches. For years, even when it was a dangerous thing to do in the south, this church has taken a stand for racial justice and has been a racially inclusive community itself. It houses a shelter for homeless people and a clinic with a doctor and dentist always on call to care for men, women, and children who have fallen through the cracks of the city's health-care system. Its preaching and worship carefully avoid any hint of sexism. It welcomes people who are openly gay and lesbian. It is almost a model for what I believe a genuinely Christian church in and for the world ought to look like. Almost.

One of the ministers of that church recently told me about a session meeting in which new elders were asked to describe the "faith journey" that had led to their being elected officers in the church. She said that one after the other they talked about how that church's stand for justice, compassion, and inclusiveness had attracted them to it, often after they had dropped out of other churches they found boring, exclusive, and irrelevant. Moving, impressive stories of deeply committed Christian men and women. But, the minister said, not one of these new elders found it necessary to mention God, Jesus Christ, the Bible, or the confessional affirmations of the church in order to talk about their own faith and life or about their understanding of the church's ministry in the city.

Then there is a more typical Presbyterian church not far from the first one. The minister there had asked me to lead a series of discussions about "what Presbyterians believe." He assured me that this church is not a fundamentalist or an "evangelical" one—just an ordinary congregation of middle-class, mostly white Christians who are good Bible-believing, loyal Presbyterians. But, he said, they are worried about the loss of membership in all the mainline churches today and disturbed about all the controversy that is tearing the Presbyterian Church apart, and he hoped that I would deal with that. I introduced this series of discussions by saying that we live in a post-Christian, multicultural, pluralistic society in which people who are different from one another have to learn to respect one another and live together in peace: people of different religions and the ever-increasing number of people with no religious faith at all; people who live by different ethical values and norms; men and women who are no longer willing to play the subservient role traditionally assigned to them; people who differ in sexual orientation, race, class, and cultural heritage. In the past, I said, we assumed that our traditional white, middle-class, Euro-American, male-defined Protestant understanding of God and Christian faith and life is or should be normative for everyone. But now we have to learn what it means to be Christians and Presbyterians in a church (and a world) that no longer belongs to people like us. A man raised his hand and was applauded by most of the people in the room when he asked, "How can we get it back again?"

What happened in these two churches is a confirmation of what Jürgen Moltmann wrote in the introductory chapter of *The Crucified God*:

> The Christian life of theologians, churches and human beings is faced more than ever today with a double crisis: *the crisis of relevance* and the *crisis of identity*. These two crises are complementary. The more theology and the

church attempt to become relevant to the problems of the present day, the more deeply they are drawn into a crisis of their own identity. The more they attempt to assert their identity in traditional dogmas, rights and moral notions, the more irrelevant and unbelievable they become. This double crisis can be more accurately described as the *identity-involvement dilemma*.[1]

Moltmann's analysis of the crisis the church faces in our time, and the concrete illustration of this crisis in the lives of the two churches I have described, define the problem I intend to address here: whether and how we can maintain Christian identity and faithfulness in a pluralistic church and society without becoming exclusive, intolerant, and irrelevant; and whether and how we can be an open, inclusive, relevant community of Christians without losing our Christian identity and authenticity.

It is not a new problem, of course, but only a new version of a problem that has confronted the church throughout its history, beginning with the struggle to define Christian faith in relation to Jews and gentiles in the church we read about in the New Testament. And Moltmann is only one of many contemporary theologians who have recognized it as the most critical theological problem of our time. Among the first to note the problem were Karl Barth and Paul Tillich. Then came George Lindbeck with the so-called Yale School, and David Tracy and the "Chicago School," and the authors of the recent torrent of books with "pluralism" in the title. They have divided up sides in their concern, above all, to maintain the distinctive identity of the Christian faith or to defend its relevance. But they all have in common their recognition that the relation between the two defines the crisis and the task of Christian faith in our post-Christian pluralistic world.

In this book I want to join in this ongoing conversation by focusing on one particular aspect of the problem and offering one set of theological resources for dealing with it.

As my introductory stories anticipate, I will discuss the problem as it affects the everyday life of the church. To use David Tracy's distinctions, I want primarily to address the "public" of ministers, theological students, and lay people in the Christian community, not the public of scholars in the wider academic community or that of our pluralistic society in general.[2] We cannot ignore these larger communities, of course, both because of what the church is called to say and do in them and because of what we have to learn from them. But everything we Christians say to the world around us will be hypocritical and unconvincing if we do not know how to deal with the problem of pluralism among ourselves. So we will be talking mostly about "us," not about "them."

More specifically, I will look at the identity-relevance issue from the particular perspective of the Reformed tradition, addressing, first of all, ministers and lay people in Presbyterian and Reformed churches (but with the conviction that the Reformed tradition is itself an ecumenical one committed to learn from and make its particular contribution to the faith and life of the larger church).

Even more specifically, I will tackle the problem from the perspective of the Reformed *confessional* tradition framed by Calvin and other Swiss Reformers at its beginning and by such contemporary theologians as Barth and Moltmann in our time. I will emphasize especially the selection of early and contemporary confessional statements and catechisms (including the ecumenical Nicene and Apostles' creeds) included in *The Book of Confessions* of the Presbyterian Church (U.S.A.) and *A Declaration of Faith*, which was adopted by the old "southern" Presbyterian Church in the United States for study and use in liturgy, and has been widely used for these purposes in the reunited Presbyterian Church. But is is important for North American Presbyterians to remember that they are a part of a worldwide community of Reformed churches that has produced a much richer confessional tradition than is suggested by the few confessional statements they have chosen to be especially authoritative for their particular denomination. We will therefore also make use of confessional statements from this broader Reformed tradition.[3]

I will approach the identity-relevance crisis that all churches face in our time from the perspective of this broad Reformed confessional tradition first of all because of my own commitment to it and my concern to remind the Presbyterian Church to which I belong that it is not this or that liberal or conservative theological position or social and political agenda but precisely our confessional tradition that defines who we are, what we believe, and how we are committed to live: To be a Christian (especially to be an ordained leader) in a Presbyterian or a Reformed church is to be "instructed," "led," and "continually

guided" by that church's confessional consensus concerning "what
Scripture leads us to believe and do."[4]

But it is not just narrow denominational loyalty or a concern to
defend theological orthodoxy that leads me to turn to the Reformed
confessional tradition for guidance in dealing with the crisis in which
we find ourselves. I believe and will argue that this tradition not only
permits but requires and enables an understanding of Christian (not
just Presbyterian–Reformed) faith and life that is both distinctively
Christian *and* open to mutually instructive dialogue and fellowship
between Christians who are different from each other, and between
Christians and non-Christians, in a pluralistic church and society.

In chapter 1 I will discuss in greater detail the identity-relevance
crisis itself. In chapters 2 and 3 I will show how the Reformed confessional tradition provides guidelines for breaking the impasse. Then
in the three remaining chapters I will demonstrate what an authentically Christian and genuinely relevant theology looks like by reclaiming and reinterpreting three central emphases of classical Reformed theology: emphasis on the sovereignty of God, emphasis on
salvation by God's grace in Jesus Christ alone, and emphasis on
Christian life in the Spirit.

Chapter One

The Double Crisis
of Identity
and Relevance

At the risk of oversimplifying and making caricatures, I intend in this chapter to describe in broad strokes ways in which some individuals and groups in the church respond to the challenge of pluralism by one-sidedly committing themselves *either* to defend the theological and ethical integrity of the church *or* to make it relevant to life in the modern world. I will argue that in choosing one alternative or the other they lose the very Christian identity or relevance that is most important to them. My purpose in this discussion is not simply to condemn inadequate ways of dealing with the identity-relevance dilemma in which we are caught but to learn from them, and point to another way that is both more faithful and more relevant.

The Quest for Christian Identity

All serious Christians seek to defend and maintain their own and the church's faithfulness and integrity. But some are convinced that to do so is to defend and maintain their "true" understanding of Christian faith and life, and of the church's mission in the world, in opposition to the "false" or "distorted" understanding of anyone inside or outside the church who differs from them. I will call these Christians "true believers."

We usually assume (as does Moltmann) that they are "evangelical" or "conservative" Christians. But people who are sure that they are true believers committed to authentic Christianity can be found in all theological camps. Some, for instance, are sure that they are the defenders of a genuinely biblical-Christian faith because they define it as belief in the deity of Jesus or faith in Jesus Christ as one's personal Lord and Savior. Others, however, are equally sure that *they* defend genuinely biblical-Christian faith because they define it as faith in Jesus Christ as the liberator of marginalized women, minorities, and the poor and oppressed. Some are sure that to be committed to authentic Christianity is to be committed to a conservative political and social agenda. But others are equally sure that it is to be committed to a liberal or liberationist agenda, and still others believe that it means belonging to a Spirit-filled, disciplined community of faithful Christians who withdraw from the public arena altogether.

In the United States today, strangely enough, the criteria for distinguishing true Christian identity are initially neither theological nor political but *sexual,* and a battle rages about whether true Christians are those who are gender-inclusive or gender-exclusive in talking about God and fellow human beings, sympathetic or hostile toward the feminist movement, for or against the inclusion of homosexual persons in the membership and leadership of the church, pro-life or pro-choice on the abortion issue. In any case, people who are sure that they represent true Christianity may be conservatives *or* liberals *or* evangelicals.

Now wherever they place themselves on the scale from left to right, true believers who are sure that their way is the only way seek first of all through private conversation, preaching and teaching, and debates in church assemblies to *persuade* others of the correctness of their position. But if they are unsuccessful, they generally choose one of two alternatives—*fight* or *flight.*

In the first case theological and ethical debates become not an attempt to persuade but a power struggle to defeat, dominate, and control those who are not on "our side" and to exclude them from having a significant voice in decisions about what the church believes and stands for.

In the second case (the flight alternative), those who are sure they represent true Christianity decide that the church has become hopelessly compromised, faithless, and disobedient, so they withdraw from the larger "false" church of uncommitted or wrongly committed

Christians to form a smaller community of *real* Christians—Christians like themselves. They are the conservative, evangelical, or liberal group within a congregation, a church in town, a group of churches in a denomination, or independent churches who withdraw from the "bureaucratic" "institutional" church altogether to proclaim themselves as those who alone stand for the true Christian position on theological, on ethical, and now above all, on gender and sexual issues.

As different as they are, true believers of all kinds who choose to defend their position by fight or by flight have more in common than they usually recognize.

First, they are suspicious and afraid of pluralism in the church, as well as in society. Those who seek faithful Christian community by *defeating those who differ* from them and those who seek it by *having as little as possible to do* with them both believe that Christian authenticity and unity can come only when *one* understanding of Christian faith and life prevails—theirs. They have in common the conviction that they have nothing to learn from people who think and live differently from them. There is neither the need nor the possibility of mutually instructive conversation; the purpose of any conversation that does take place is only to defend one's own position and to criticize and reject other positions.

Second, those who pursue both the fight and flight ways of defending and maintaining authentic Christian faith and life are self-defeating. Those conservatives, evangelicals, or liberals who are convinced that they already know what faithfulness to the gospel requires them to think, say, and do not only cut themselves off from the self-criticism and correction that could come from a genuine two-way conversation with fellow Christians and others different from them; they also cut themselves off from the self-criticism and correction that could come from the very gospel they themselves want above all to defend. Their final loyalty is not to the Christian gospel itself but to their particular interpretation of it.

Finally, both strategies are ironically self-contradictory. Both those who seek to defend authentic Christianity by attacking and defeating their unbelieving or wrong-believing and disobedient enemies in church and world, and those who build a defensive wall around themselves to associate only with others like themselves, mark a strange contrast with the Christ they want to serve. Christ came not to lord it over others but to give himself for them. He was the *friend* of those whom righteous insiders rejected. He *loved* his enemies and sought to reconcile and include, not defeat or exclude them. Both the fight-and-flight strategies to defend authentic Christian identity and faithfulness lose the very thing that is most important them.

The Quest for Christian Relevance

A second kind of Christian is the kind who wants above all to stand for an open and relevant rather than a closed and exclusive understanding of Christian faith and life. If the most common strategy of "true believers" is either fight or flight, the most common strategy of these Christians is some form of reductionistic accommodation or pluralistic inclusivism. I will call them "reductionists" (though they would never call themselves that) and "pluralists."

Reductionists

Reductionists are Christians who seek to make the Christian faith relevant by placing it in service of what they believe are the best (or at least the most prevalent) values and goals of the society in which they live. They may side with true believers of one kind or another in dealing with particular issues facing the church, but while true believers claim to be guided first of all by the promises and demands of biblical-Christian faith, reductionists deliberately or unconsciously "let the world set the agenda."

It is usually assumed that this is a "liberal" strategy but, like true believers, reductionists too may be liberals, conservatives, or evangelicals. In the North American Presbyterian Church today, for instance, they are those *liberals* (mostly among the church's leadership?) who identify the gospel and mission of the church with programs sponsored by the moderate or left wing of the Democratic party. They want the government to legislate social, political, and economic justice for all—while insisting that decisions about personal morality are a matter of individual personal preference. But reductionists may also be *conservatives* (most grass-roots church members?) who identify the gospel and mission of the church with programs of moderate or right-wing Republicans. They emphasize individual initiative, responsibility, and self-help; and they oppose "government interference"—except perhaps to enforce their own standards of personal morality and "family values."

There are also reductionist *evangelicals*. They are those evangelicals who have little to say about the costly demands of Christian discipleship and social justice, but proclaim a gospel that promises to solve people's personal problems, give them everything they want, make them happy, healthy, and wealthy in this life and save them in the next—a gospel that is only a pious version of the possessive individualism, narcissism, and consumerism that are characteristic of modern secular society.[1]

Liberal, conservative, or evangelical, reductionists may defend their position with biblical and theological arguments, but they use scripture and talk about God, Christ, or the Holy Spirit only to validate the right- or left-wing political ideology, the ethical values and moral standards, or the individualistic commitment to personal happiness and success they already had before they began to think as Christians.

But that means that, like true believers, reductionists of various kinds are suspicious of genuine pluralism in church and society. They too believe that their way is the only true way, and are sure that they have nothing to learn from fellow Christians and others who are different from them. For them too the purpose of biblical-theological (and political) discussion is only to defend their agenda and discredit that of others.

They are also like true believers in that in their own way they too are caught in a strategy for relating gospel and world that is self-defeating and self-contradictory. They want above all to be relevant to the pluralistic world around them, yet they make themselves essentially superfluous and irrelevant because they have nothing to say that is different from what is already being said (perhaps better said) by the Democratic, Republican, or Marxist party platforms; by the Boy Scouts, Rotary Club, or Chamber of Commerce; by one or another of the secular advocacy groups that defend the interests of some particular segment of society; or by those who sponsor this or that technique of therapeutic self-fulfillment. All Christian reductionists have to offer *to* the world is a religious echo of one or another of the rival alternatives they have imported *from* the world. They make themselves irrelevant precisely in their attempt to be relevant, and contribute to rather than healing the divisiveness and hostility between various groups and ideologies in the world around them.

Having let the world, or some part of it, set the agenda, reductionists cut themselves off from the discovery of a really interesting and truly relevant *alternative* to all the warring groups and ideologies around them. They cut themselves off from a *distinctively Christian* understanding of justice, freedom, peace, and human wholeness. They withhold from the society they want to serve one of the things it most desperately needs to learn: the Christian understanding of the *inseparable connection* between true individual morality and self-fulfillment on the one hand, and life lived for the common good of the whole human community on the other. Above all they give up a distinctively Christian hope in what the *living God*—not just liberal, conservative, or evangelical Christians—can and will do for the liberation, reconciliation, and renewal of people in a pluralistic church and world.

Pluralists

A second strategy for seeking a relevant Christian faith and church is to acknowledge, claim, and celebrate the religious, cultural, ethical, and ideological diversity that both true believers and reductionists fear. It is the strategy of Christians I have called "pluralists." They believe that if we really want to discover the truth about God and God's will for our personal and corporate life in the church, and if we really want the church to be an instrument of God's justice, compassion, and reconciliation in the world, we must be a community that welcomes and enters into dialogue with people inside and outside the church who are different from one another. Only in this way can we hope to discover truth that is greater than any of us can know alone and overcome the differences that divide us into warring camps.

An indication of support for this strategy is the popularity in our time of what has become an almost mandatory slogan constantly repeated in sermons, editorials, and church study papers and debates: "Unity in diversity." It is a good slogan for Christians who confess that the church is one body with many members, and who want both to affirm pluralism and to heal the divisiveness it creates. But to affirm "unity in diversity" does not automatically solve the problem; it can only underline it. This becomes obvious when we look carefully at what seem to me to be the two main ways the slogan is usually interpreted.

On the one hand, there are theologians, ministers, and lay people who believe that the church should welcome the diverse views and commitments of different kinds of people but seek through dialogue to discover the common religious sensitivity and moral and social vision they all share despite their differences—an underlying consensus that includes but expands the limited insights, needs, and concerns of any one group. The movement here is from everything particular, concrete, and specific that *distinguishes* people from one another to the general, abstract, and universal affirmations that *unite* them. For want of a better name for those who choose this strategy, I will call them "common core" pluralists.

On the other hand, others who seek unity in diversity believe that it is found in embracing diversity itself. For them reconciliation and unity are not achieved by seeking some common universal agreement *behind* or *under* the differences that divide people. These goals are achieved rather by the mutual acceptance of people *in* and *with* their differences, no "preferential option" given to any one group, no one group's claiming that its way is the only way, the diverse perspectives and commitments of all people treated with equal respect. Those who make this the goal of pluralistic conversation are often accused of being theological and ethical relativists, but they too are passionately committed people, people committed to do everything they can to create an inclusive church that works for an inclusive society. I will call them "inclusivists."

"Unity in diversity" is a good slogan. But I believe that neither the common-core nor the inclusivist strategy can be successful in achieving this goal because in different ways both of them force us finally to *choose between* unity and diversity.

Think first of the common-core strategy that welcomes diversity, then seeks through dialogue to discover behind, under, or above it a common moral, religious, and social vision everyone can affirm.

In a dialogue between men and women, and between people of different races, classes, and cultures, the common-core strategy asks participants to give up talking too specifically about their *particular* experience, needs, and goals and to think of themselves as generic human beings who should love and accept one another since "we all share a common humanity and deep down we all want the same thing." (This is a common strategy used by those who want to silence the "strident" or "one-sided" voices of black, feminist, or Latin American liberation theologians: "After all, *all* of us are poor and oppressed in one way or another.")

When the conversation becomes a religious or interreligious one, the common-core strategy requires people to give up or remain silent about the particular persons, historical events, and theological convictions that have shaped their particular faith—or at best to think of these only as examples or illustrations of more general religious truth arrived at by different paths and expressed in different ways—in order to discover a common universal faith in a "divine Reality" (John Hick) that offends no one and which everyone can accept. ("We Christians must not talk too much about God's self-revelation in Christ," a seminary student wrote, "because that arrogantly cuts off dialogue with people of other religious traditions." Presumably that means we should also ask Jews, Muslims, and others to be silent about what is most important in *their* communities of faith.)

Whatever the context, participants in a pluralistic dialogue are asked to give up the very social, historical, and theological particularity that makes them who they are for the sake of a general abstract unity that requires them to *forget* or *deny* who they are.

In other words, in a strangely self-contradictory and self-defeating way common-core pluralists seek reconciliation and unity *at the expense of* acknowledgment of real diversity, a *false* reconciliation and unity that tries to cover over instead of dealing honestly with differences. In the end, such a strategy can only *intensify* differences that alienate people from each other. Especially in light of the fact that the content of "universal religious faith" and "the goals of our common humanity" are always defined according to the presuppositions and self-interest of representatives of one particular group (usually those with the most power) who claim that what is normative for them is normative for everyone.[2]

If real reconciliation and unity are to come at all, they can come only when people openly *claim* their particular religious faith and ethical commitments and *assert* their needs and demands as men or women of a particular race, class, and culture, yet seek to understand and to be with and for others who *really are* different from them. But that is just what common-core pluralism fears and tries to avoid.

It seems, then, that the second kind of pluralists, the inclusivists, have a more promising strategy for pluralistic dialogue and fellowship.

Inclusivists want to affirm and preserve rather than overcome diversity. They want a church that demonstrates in its own life and sponsors in the world a tolerant openness in which people who are different from one another listen to one another, learn from one another, accept and include one another *in* and *with* their differences.

But when Christians and churches committed to inclusiveness face the implications of their position, they too find themselves caught in a self-contradictory and self-defeating dilemma. Does inclusiveness mean, for instance, that the church should welcome and take with equal seriousness the claims of Christians who reject *and* those who defend a patriarchal, hierarchical understanding of God and human relationships in family and society? Should we equally affirm and welcome those who believe that Jesus is one of many ways *and* those who insist that he is the *only* way? Should we recognize as acceptable options the position of those who are for *and* those who are against the program of the "religious right" regarding prayer and Bible reading in public assemblies, for *and* against abortion and the inclusion of homosexual people in church and society? That is not what is intended by most seminary students, ministers, and church members I know who are committed to "inclusiveness." They differ from traditional Christians only in their decisions about *which* people and *which* points of view should be included and which, therefore, excluded.

Inclusivists do not in fact really believe in the wide-open inclusivism they theoretically defend. Instead of achieving the unity and reconciliation they seek, they end up fanning the flames of a war between "true believers" on the right and on the left. Moreover, if they are asked just *how they decide* who and what is included or excluded, they find themselves in a trap. They cannot justify their position by an appeal to scripture and the promises and requirement of the Christian gospel because their inclusivist position proclaims their acceptance of all points of view, including interpretations of scripture and the gospel different from their own. But then they are left finally to appeal only to their personal preferences and ideological commitments — which according to their own inclusivist position can claim no more authority than those of anyone else.

The truth is that no one really believes that just any and every religious, political, and ethical option is possible for Christians, the church, and human society. We all make judgments about what is possible or impossible, required or forbidden, acceptable or unacceptable if we want a truly Christian church and a truly human society in which diverse people live together in unity and peace. A genuinely relevant Christian theology and ethic will provide some criteria and guidelines for making such judgments. But neither common-core nor inclusivist pluralists can do this, because in different ways they *give up* the quest for a distinctively biblical-Christian contribution to the task of achieving unity in diversity.

Is there any way out of the mess in which we find ourselves? Is it possible to understand Christian faith and life in such a way that it is authentically Christian without being arrogant, exclusive, and irrelevant and at the same time open, inclusive, and relevant without compromising or sacrificing Christian identity and integrity? Anyone who looks at the self-defeating and self-contradictory alternatives we have discussed knows that there are no easy answers. But in the chapters that follow I will argue that the Reformed confessional tradition points the way toward the discovery of an understanding of Christian faith and life that is (1) authentically and unreservedly Christian and *just for that reason* open to pluralistic conversation and community; and (2) truly relevant *just because* it openly and unapologetically seeks to make a distinctively biblical-Christian contribution to the quest for unity in diversity in our pluralistic church and society.[3]

Chapter Two

The Religious Relativism of the Reformed Tradition

Karl Barth began a series of lectures on the Apostles' Creed in 1946 with these words: "Dogmatics is the science in which the church, in accordance with the state of its knowledge at different times, takes account of the content of its proclamation critically, that is, by the standard of holy scripture and under the guidance of its confessions."[1]

In the introduction of his 1992 book *Processive Revelation*, Benjamin Reist, professor of theology at the Graduate Theological Union in California, argues that Barth's definition of the task of theology is still valid. In our time too theology has what Reist calls "three normative components": biblical base, confessional tradition, and "the state of the church's knowledge at different times" (the historical-social context in which the church seeks in every new time, place, and situation to understand the Bible and be guided by the church's confessions). But, Reist argues, Barth was so afraid that preoccupation with context would undermine the priority of scripture and confessional tradition that he did not pay enough attention to it. Our task today is to take *all three* components more seriously than Barth was able to do: "One may not deal with any one of them without touching the other two, and one may begin the discussion with any one of them so long as the other two are taken into account."[2] Nevertheless, Reist insists, we must pay special attention to the third component, which

Barth neglected: "Whenever and wherever the gospel of Jesus Christ is a living reality, there it will manifest the marks of authentic relation to the *contexts* within which it is heard."[3]

I believe that Reist is correct in his description of the task of theology in our time. I believe that only such an understanding of the task can enable us to deal effectively with what Moltmann calls the crisis of identity and relevance in the life of the church today—the crisis exposed by the various attempts we have discussed to maintain Christian identity at the expense of relevance, openness, and inclusiveness; or to be relevant, open, and inclusive at the expense of compromising Christian identity. Moreover, I believe that Christians in the Presbyterian–Reformed tradition do not have to look around for a new theological base to deal with the crisis. They have only to take their own confessional heritage seriously, for in it respect for the authority of scripture, respect for Christian tradition, and faithful response to historical-cultural context are inextricably related in a way that both requires and enables an understanding of Christian faith and life that is at once authentically Christian and at the same time open to dialogue and fellowship with fellow Christians and others who are different from us in a pluralistic church and world.

In this and the next chapter I will argue that the way Reist's three "normative components" are related in the Reformed tradition provide the *method* for achieving such an understanding of Christian faith and life. Then we will use this method to deal with what I believe are some of the most important issues Christians must face in our pluralistic situation.

I want to emphasize that I have no interest in contributing to the self-glorification that is characteristic of some who belong to Presbyterian or Reformed churches. When Reformed Christians have been true to their own confessional heritage, they have never claimed to know something about Christian faith and life that no one else knows or to have *the* correct theology. They have always sought to represent an ecumenical Christianity that is open to recognize their own faith in other Christian traditions, and eager to participate in conversation with them that is mutually instructive and corrective. An authentic understanding of their own Reformed tradition forbids complacent self-congratulation and requires self-criticism and commitment to reform *themselves* before they presume to reform *others*.

Nevertheless, it is true that Presbyterian and Reformed churches are committed to a unique way of relating scripture, confessional tradition, and social-historical context. Without claiming that their way of doing it is the only way, I believe that it provides the most promising way of resolving the identity-relevance dilemma that is tearing us apart. We can best define this way by describing the unique position churches in the Reformed tradition occupy between so-called free churches on the left and other confessional churches such as the Roman Catholic and Lutheran on the right.[4]

The Uniqueness of the
Reformed Confessional Tradition

In contrast to free churches and like other confessional churches, Reformed churches are precisely *confessional* churches, churches that understand the task of interpreting scripture and defining the meaning of Christian faith and life to be that of a *community* of Christians. Confessions of faith, creeds, and catechisms are by definition officially adopted consensus statements by which a Christian community makes clear to itself and to the world what the members of that community believe and resolve to do *together*.

People who decide to belong to confessional churches do not have to, nor (if they are faithful members) do they attempt to interpret scripture and Christian faith and life according to their own personal religious experience or ethical and political preferences. Neither do they have to or try to do this only in the company of others who are like them in gender, race, class, cultural heritage, and political inclination. Free from both the loneliness and the arrogance of trying to figure out everything themselves, they subject themselves to the guidance, judgment, and correction of *their church's* interpretation of scripture and what it calls them to believe and do. That is as true of Presbyterian–Reformed Christians as it is of those who belong to other confessional churches.

But Reformed churches differ from other confessional churches in two notable ways. First, Reformed confessional statements do not come "from above," on the authority of any individual (whether pope or theologian—including Calvin) or on the authority of an elite group (whether bishops, church bureaucracy, or the most powerful liberal or conservative theological party in the church). Reformed confessions come "from below"—from the members of the church themselves and elected representatives responsible to them. In the words of Barth, Reformed confessional statements are "the result of discussion and subsequent voting carried on with wide open doors."[5] We may add that this discussion includes both men and women of every race and cultural background belonging to the church involved, with various theological and political points of view; and that in the final voting there is a parity of clergy and laity.

Reformed Christians operate by this democratic process not because they identify the will of God with that of the majority of the people, but because they believe that we are more likely to discern the truth, promises, and demands of the gospel when there is full, free public debate about what the Holy Spirit speaking through scripture is leading the church to say and do, even though it may not be in agreement with the personal preferences or serve the self-interest of any one group within the church.

Respect for the authority of the *church,* under the authority of *scripture,* with openness to listen to people who represent *various social contexts*—all three are built into the democratic process by which confessional statements are formulated and adopted in Reformed churches. Because of the composition of the membership and/or leadership in particular Reformed communities, one or more of these three components may sometimes be slighted. But Reformed churches are distinguished from other confessional churches first of all in that their "from below" process of producing confessional statements both allows and requires all three.

A second difference between churches in the Reformed tradition and other confessional churches—and in the context of our present discussion the most important—is the *great number* of Reformed confessional statements. Other confessional traditions have been content with only a few official confessions formulated by a few people, within narrow geographical or historical limits. All the great Lutheran confessions, for instance, were written either by Luther himself or by one of his immediate followers, in Germany, between 1529 and 1580. Authoritative Roman Catholic teaching comes from the ancient church councils, from the Council of Trent, or from Rome, where the contribution of Catholic churches around the world may be given consideration but can also be overruled.

From its very beginning, however, wherever the Reformed

movement has spread, Reformed Christians have made new confessions of faith—first city by city, then country by country. In the sixteenth and seventeenth centuries, confessions of Bern, Basel, Zurich, and Geneva were followed by one or more confessions of regional Reformed churches in Switzerland, France, Germany, Belgium, Holland, Hungary, and Scotland. For reasons we need not consider here, this great surge of confession writing came to an end by the end of the seventeenth century.[6] But the twentieth century has seen a revival of the original impulse of Reformed churches to produce new confessional statements. More than thirty of them, adopted by Reformed churches in all parts of the world, are included in Lukas Vischer's collection in his *Reformed Witness Today*.[7]

When one reads these documents, written by many different people in different times, places, and situations, one finds a remarkable consistency in their recognizably and distinctively Reformed understanding of Christian faith and life. From the earliest to the most recent, for instance, they all confess faith in one triune God. All express the same faith in Jesus Christ as our one Lord and Savior. All acknowledge the unique authority of scripture. All emphasize God's sovereign claim on both our personal lives and our corporate life in church and society. All emphasize the inseparable connection between the justifying and the sanctifying grace of God—grace that not only forgives and saves but also enables and requires lives of thankful Christian discipleship. All have the same theology of Word and Sacrament.

But there are significant differences too—not only differences that result from saying the same thing in different ways but also substantial differences in interpretation of what scripture leads Christians to believe and say and do. They differ, for instance, in their understanding of predestination or election (a doctrine central to them all). Contemporary Reformed confessions differ from earlier ones in what they say about marriage and divorce, the role of women in the church, and the relation between church and state. In marked contrast to contemporary confessional statements, those of the sixteenth and seventeenth centuries show little interest in evangelism and the mission of the church in and for the world.

Why have churches in the Reformed tradition produced such a multiplicity of confessions that cannot always be harmonized with

one another? Why their refusal to recognize any one of them or selection of them as having the authority to speak for all Reformed
Christians, always, everywhere? Why their openness to change, even
if it means calling into question or actually contradicting what faithful Reformed Christians in other times and places have taught—
including Calvin himself and the other original reformers?

The answer lies in what Reformed churches understand their
confessional statements to be. Karl Barth was not just expressing his
own theology but making a statement of historical fact when he said
in a lecture delivered in 1925 that for Reformed Christians confessions of faith are by definition "fragmentary insights" into God's revelation in Jesus Christ which are "given for the moment," "formulated
by a Christian community within a geographically limited area," and
authoritative "only until further action."[8] This does not mean that Reformed Christians believe they have nothing to learn from past confessional statements, which may in fact have long-lasting authority
for them. But it does mean that, as Barth said, in the Reformed tradition all confessions, old or new, have only a provisional, temporary,
and relative authority, and are therefore always subject to revision and
correction. That is why Barth could speak of the "religious relativism" of the Reformed confessional tradition.[9]

We will look at this religious relativism in some detail, not only
because we discover in it what distinguishes churches in the Reformed tradition from churches in other confessional traditions, but
because I believe that to claim and celebrate it is to discover the connection between biblical base, confessional tradition, and social-
historical context required of a theology that is both faithfully Christian and genuinely relevant in our pluralistic church and society.

The Religious Relativism of the
Reformed Confessional Tradition

At first glance the relativism of the Reformed tradition frightens
conservatives and pleases liberals. But both the fear on the one side
and the glee on the other are proved premature when we understand
three reasons for it, all of which are either presupposed or specifically
stated in Reformed confessions themselves.

Human Limitations and Sinfulness

In the Reformed tradition, confessions have a temporary, provisional, relative authority (and are therefore subject to revision and correction) because all confessions are the work of limited, fallible, sinful human beings and churches. Throughout their history Reformed Christians have openly acknowledged with the Westminster Confession of 1647 that "All synods or councils since the apostles' times, whether general or particular, may err, and many have erred; therefore they are not to be made the rule of faith and practice, but to be used as a help in both" (ch. XXXIII.3). "The purest churches under heaven are subject both to mixture and error" (ch. XXVII.5).

It is important to note that such statements apply not only to other churches but to the "synods or councils" of Reformed churches too, the Westminster Assembly included. The freedom to make such a confession is especially important now that we recognize how historically and culturally conditioned were those who wrote and adopted confessional statements in the past.

The large number of Reformed confessions is evidence that Reformed churches have always sought to bring the gospel to bear on the specific theological, moral, and political issues that have arisen in new historical and social contexts. But the here-and-now character of Reformed confessions also means that their understanding of the gospel has sometimes been *distorted* by the context in which they have borne witness to it. So, for instance, the great classical confessions of Reformed churches in the sixteenth and seventeenth centuries were written before the discoveries of modern science and reflect an outdated understanding of the structure of the world, its natural and historical processes, and the relation of God to them (just as our modern confessions will one day seem outdated and "primitive" to future generations). The confessions of every age have often assumed that the prevailing patterns of sexual, familial, and social life were God-willed, and have been unable and unwilling to grasp parts of the biblical witness to God's will for human life that might call them into question. Those who wrote and members of Reformed churches who have adopted confessional statements have often been more influenced than they realized by their vested self-interest in preserving a social and political status quo.

Many conservative Reformed Christians today become confused, angry, and defensive when they hear that what they have believed to be trustworthy witnesses to the truth about God and God's will for their personal and familial lives, and for human society, are so historically and culturally conditioned. But *their own confessional standards* acknowledge themselves to be the work of limited, fallible, sinful human beings. *Their own confessions* give them the freedom and responsibility to confess the historically and culturally conditioned character of what their church has taught about God and the will of God, and to think and act in new ways even if they are different from what faithful Reformed Christians before them have believed and said and done. That does not mean they have to reject and throw out everything their traditional confessional statements have taught, but it does mean that they are free and responsible to confess that even long-held, commonly accepted ways of thinking about God, the world, and human life are "subject both to mixture and error" and therefore open to revision and correction. To do so is not to compromise or sacrifice their Reformed heritage; it is to have the courage to live by it.

On the other hand, more liberal members of Reformed churches are *glad* to confess the limited understanding, fallibility, sinfulness, and historically and culturally conditioned character of their church's earlier confessions. They want the church to bear witness to what the promises and demands of the gospel mean for *our* time, in light of modern scientific and philosophical learning, in response to the multireligious and multicultural pluralistic world in which we have to learn what it means for *us* to be Christians. They seek alternatives to traditional concepts of God and human society, openness to new patterns of sexual and familial relationships, and new ways of organizing our economic and political life together.

Such Christians are more faithful to the Reformed tradition than those who want only to hold on to and defend "what our church has always believed and taught." But if these liberals are truly committed to the Reformed tradition, they will confess that *they too* are fallible, sinful human beings of limited wisdom and virtue. They will confess that also *their* understanding of God and the will of God for human life is shaped not only by new insights into the meaning of the gospel but also by *their* religious, philosophical, and ideological presuppositions; by the prevailing or emerging patterns of sexual and family life that seem normal, acceptable, or preferable in *their* time and place; and by *their* personal or corporate self-interest. They will confess, in other words, that like traditional Reformed Christians before and around them, what they believe about Christian faith and life is also historically and culturally conditioned. This does not mean that everything they believe and stand for will later be shown to be wrong, but it does mean that they will modestly confess that also *their* understanding of the gospel is "subject both to mixture and error."

According to the Reformed tradition that keeps producing new confessions for every new time, place, and situation, the theological and ethical insights of *all* Christians (conservative and liberal, of both genders of every race, class and culture, past *and* present) are the historically and socially conditioned insights of limited, fallible, sinful human beings and therefore subject to criticism, revision, and correction.

But if that is the case, how then can we know and say *anything* trustworthy about God and what Christians are to believe and do? For Reformed Christians the answer lies in a second reason for the plurality of confessions in their theological tradition and therefore their "religious relativism."

The Higher Authority of Scripture

In the Reformed tradition, confessions have a temporary, provisional, and relative authority (and are therefore subject to revision and correction) because they acknowledge the higher authority of scripture. The following statement from the preface to the original version of the Scots Confession of 1560 is an example of many similar statements that can be found throughout the confessional literature of Reformed churches:[10]

> We protest that if any man will note in this confession of ours any article or sentence repugnant to God's holy word, that it would please him of his gentleness and for Christian charity's sake to admonish us of the same in writing; and we upon our honor and fidelity, by God's grace do promise unto him satisfaction from the mouth of God, that is from his holy scripture, or else reformation of that which he shall prove to be amiss.

Reformed confessions, in other words, *relativize themselves*. They themselves confess that no single old or new confessional statement, and no collection of such statements, can ever have the last and definitive word. All these statements express the church's faith only in a particular time and place and are always subject to criticism and correction in light of the word of God in scripture that is the enduring norm of the church's faith and life in *every* time and place.

This Reformed commitment to what is called "the scripture principle" has of course always raised the question of the right *interpretation* of scripture. But Reformed Christians today have to deal especially with two big problems that those who lived in the sixteenth and seventeenth centuries were only beginning to be aware of. The first we have already mentioned: How can we avoid reading into scripture, or judging it by, our own culturally and historically conditioned insights and self-interest? The second is: How should we deal with the historically conditioned character of scripture itself? How can we discern the word and work of God for our time in a book written by and for ancient Near Eastern people who had a predominantly hierarchical and patriarchal understanding of God and human society, who bore witness to their faith with a prescientific worldview, and who did not even dream of all the complex problems we have to face in our modern technological society? How are we to distinguish in the Bible between what is the will of God for the lives of all people in all times and places and what, though it may have been the will of God for people "back then and there," no longer applies to us?

Reformed Christians today are as perplexed by such questions as anyone else. But I believe the Reformed confessional tradition gives us some rules for the proper interpretation of scripture that provide more help in dealing with these problems than we often recognize and utilize. The rules do not tell us everything we need to know about the hermeneutical task today, nor do they automatically provide the "right" answer to the hotly debated theological and ethical questions that threaten to split the church in our time. They are rules of biblical interpretation Reformed Christians have agreed to abide by when they talk to one another about controversial issues, not rules that determine who is going to win. I want briefly to comment on some of the most important of them because I believe that we find in them some very specific guidelines for discovering the relation between biblical base, church tradition, and historical context that is necessary if we are to be both faithfully Christian and relevant in our pluralistic church and society today.

Scripture Interprets Scripture

That scripture is interpreted by other scripture is sometimes incorrectly called *the* Reformed principle of biblical interpretation, but it is a rule that is regularly mentioned in both older and contemporary Reformed confessions.[11] It says that when we encounter difficult passages of scripture or passages the interpretation of which is controversial, we are to (1) compare them with other passages that throw a different or more light on the question at hand (Second Helvetic Confession, chap. II: "like and unlike passages"); and (2) seek to understand them in light of the total message of scripture, including parts that may not specifically deal with the question at hand. This is a safeguard against the perennial tendency of all individuals and groups to see and quote only passages of scripture that confirm what they already think and want the Bible to say, to ignore or reject other passages of scripture, and to let a few passages on a particular issue obscure what the biblical message as a whole tells us about God and God's will for our lives. A corollary of this rule in our pluralistic situation is that if it is really the will and work of God we seek to discern and not just the stamp of approval on our own personal and social biases, we must be willing to interpret it in conversation with people who are different from us—people who of course have their biases too, but who may help us to see things in the Word of God we are unable or reluctant to hear and see from our particular perspective. (In my opinion, this rule would be of enormous help to us today as we struggle with controversial issues such as that of homosexuality in church and society.)

The Christological Principle

Scripture is to be interpreted in light of the central revelation of God in Jesus Christ. "When controversy arises about the right understanding of any passage or sentence of Scripture, or for the reformation of any abuse within the Kirk of God, we ought not so much to ask what men have said or done before us, as . . . what Christ Jesus himself did and commanded" (Scots Confession, chap. XVIII).

But when something is brought before us by our pastors or by others, which brings us closer to Christ, and in accordance with God's word is more conducive to mutual friendship and Christian love than the interpretation now presented, we will gladly accept it and will not limit the course of the Holy Spirit, which does not go backwards toward the flesh but always forward towards the image of Jesus Christ our Lord. (Confession of the Synod of Bern, 1532)

Although the earliest Reformed confessions (following Calvin himself)[12] acknowledged this christological rule of interpretation, it was generally forgotten in the theology and confessions of seventeenth-century Reformed orthodoxy. Especially under the influence of Karl Barth, however, it has been more consistently recognized and applied in the twentieth century than ever before. "Jesus Christ, as he is attested for us in Holy Scripture, is the one Word of God which we have to hear and which we have to trust and obey" (Declaration of Barmen). "The Bible is to be interpreted in the light of its witness to God's work of reconciliation in Christ" (Confession of 1967, *Book of Confessions* 9.29). "When we encounter apparent tension and conflicts in what scripture teaches us to believe and do the final appeal must be made to the authority of Christ" (Declaration of Faith, 6.3).

This christological principle of interpretation has proved especially helpful as the church has struggled with contemporary issues such as that of women's place in church and society, justice for the poor and oppressed, and treatment of others who have been forgotten or excluded.

The Law of Love

Scripture is to be interpreted according to the law of love. This is another rule regularly mentioned in early Reformed confessions such as the Scots (chap. XVIII) and Second Helvetic (chap. II), but which was also forgotten in confessions representing seventeenth-century orthodoxy. I take it to be a warning that no interpretation of scripture that shows hostility or indifference toward any person or group can be a correct interpretation of the Word of the God whose will for our lives is summarized in the command to love God and our neighbors as ourselves. A corollary for our time is that it is not possible to love people who are different from us without getting to know them, listening to and learning from them, and willing only their good whether or not we agree with what they believe, say, and do.

The Rule of Faith

Scripture is to be interpreted with respect for the church's interpretation of it. This rule, also mentioned in the Scots (chap. XVIII) and Second Helvetic (chap. II) confessions, is summarized by the Declaration of Faith in this way: "Listening with respect to fellow believers past and present, we anticipate that the Holy Spirit will guide us to interpret faithfully the Word of God for our time and place" (Declaration of Faith, 6.3).

According to Reformed tradition, the Holy spirit enables us truly to hear and understand the word of God in scripture. But the Spirit was promised to the whole Christian community, not just to individual Christians. Faithful Christians in the past, long before any of us came along, came together in the church to seek the Spirit's guidance, and faithful Christians gathered in the church today still do so. Whether old or new, the church's interpretation is always subject to criticism and correction in light of further study of scripture itself. But we are more likely to interpret it rightly, and to avoid confusing the guidance of the Spirit with our own personal and social biases, when we first of all listen carefully and respectfully to the consensus of the church concerning what scripture requires us to believe and do, not deciding too quickly that it is outdated or wrong.

Respect for Literary
and Historical Context

Scripture is to be interpreted in light of the various literary forms and social-historical contexts in which it was written. This is not a new principle of interpretation. Calvin and early Reformed confessions applied it within the limits of the scientific and historical knowledge and exegetical tools available to them.[13] But it is especially emphasized by contemporary Reformed confessions. The Confession of 1967 puts it this way:

> The Scriptures, given under the guidance of the Holy
> Spirit, are nevertheless the words of men, conditioned by
> the language, thought forms, and literary fashions of the

places and times at which they were written. They reflect views of life, history, and the cosmos which were then current. The church, therefore, has an obligation to approach the Scriptures with literary and historical understanding (*BC,* 9.29).

Or, according to the Declaration of Faith (6.3): "God has chosen to address his inspired word to us through diverse and varied human writings. Therefore we use the best available methods to understand them in their historical and cultural setting and the literary forms in which they are cast."[14]

Three things are notable about such statements: (1) They openly acknowledge the contextual character of the biblical writings themselves as well as that of all interpretations of them. (2) They give us a theological, not just a scientific-academic, reason for a contextual interpretation of scripture: *"God has chosen"* to reveal God's self to us in the witness of those ancient Jews and Christians. Precisely when we want to hear the word of God in scripture, we must be willing to hear it in and through the historically and culturally conditioned form in which it comes to us. (3) With the Confession of 1967, contemporary Reformed confessions generally emphasize that "As God has spoken his word in diverse cultural situations, . . . he will continue to speak through the scriptures in a changing world in every form of human culture" (*BC,* 9.29).

I emphasize especially this third point, because it points to a third reason for the multiplicity and "relativism" of Reformed confession.

Faith in a Living God

In the Reformed tradition confessions have a temporary, provisional, and relative authority (and are therefore subject to revision and correction) because scripture bears witness to a living God who not only spoke and acted in the distant past but continues to speak and act in every new time and place. The reason Reformed churches have never been content simply to repeat and defend confessional statements made in other times and places but have kept producing new ones is not only that they know about the limited wisdom, fallibility, and sinfulness of those who wrote and churches that adopted them. Nor is the reason just that they have acknowledged that all the church's confessions are subject to criticism and correction in light of fresh interpretation of the word of God in the Bible according to certain agreed-on rules of interpretation. There is another reason: They have continually asked in every new time and place what the living God we come to know in scripture is saying and doing *here* and *now,* and what we have to say and do if we are to be faithful and obedient Christians in *our* particular time and place—even if it means saying and doing things that may seem strange or shocking when compared with what Christians in other times and places have felt called to say and do.

When we come to speak of faith in the living God who not only spoke and acted in an earlier time but continues to speak and act, we come to what I believe is the very heart of the faith of Reformed Christians, the reason behind both the other reasons for the "religious relativism" of the Reformed confessional tradition, and the most fundamental reason for its unique understanding of the relationship between biblical authority, church tradition, and social-historical context.

But if Reformed churches today are to be faithful to their own biblically based tradition and speak a genuinely relevant word in the pluralistic context in which we live, I believe we must answer more carefully and consistently than have either past or contemporary confessions of faith the question on which everything else depends: "Who is this living God?"

Chapter Three

Reformed by Faith in the Living Triune God

Who is the living God whose word and work Christians in the Reformed confessional tradition seek to discern afresh in every new time and place, and to whom they seek to bear faithful and obedient witness in their particular time and place? With Christians of all other Christian traditions, Reformed Christians have always answered this question by confessing their faith in one triune God who is Father, Son, and Holy Spirit. But I believe the validity of all the claims we have made about the Reformed tradition is called into question precisely by the classical doctrine of the Trinity as defined in the early Reformed confessions of the sixteenth and seventeenth centuries, and to some extent also by revisions of it in twentieth-century Reformed confessions. I believe that it is precisely with the criticism and reformation of their Trinitarian theology that Reformed Christians today must begin if they are to be open to hear and live by the promises and demands of the living God of scripture in our present social and historical context. That is the task we will address in this chapter.

We do not have to go about it without help, of course. A number of contemporary theologians, representing different Christian traditions, are also working at a new and "reformed" doctrine of the Trinity: Reformed theologians such as Jürgen Moltmann, Daniel L. Migliore, and William C. Placher; Roman Catholics such as Karl Rahner, Leonardo Boff, and Catherine Mowry LaCugna; Lutherans such as Eberhard Jüngel, Wolfhart Pannenberg, Robert Jensen, and Ted Peters.[1] I will not attempt to compare and summarize their work, but I will be depending on it to do three things: First, I will summarize in broad strokes what I consider to be the most critical issues and problems raised by the traditional Western doctrine of the Trinity expressed in early Reformed confessions of the sixteenth and seventeenth centuries. Then I will look at the way contemporary Reformed confessions have begun to deal with these issues. Finally I will reclaim two ancient rules for Trinitarian thinking that I believe can help us move beyond both earlier and more recent confessions toward a more consistently Trinitarian understanding of God that is faithfully Christian, authentically Reformed, and genuinely relevant in our pluralistic church and society.

The Trinity in
Early Reformed Confessions

When we look at early Reformed confessions, we can see that, with minor variations (and some exceptions), they have several things in common:[2]

First, in all of them the doctrine of the Trinity is preceded by a monotheistic philosophical definition of God and God's attributes. Following medieval tradition, they define God first of all as the self-existent origin or first cause of all things who can be described with a list of adjectives derived either from the negation of everything creaturely and earthly (the *via negativa*), or from reflection on the highest and best we can imagine (the *via eminentiae*). God is thus the Supreme Being, eternal, omnipotent, infinite, immeasurable, incomprehensible, immutable, immortal, immense, self-sufficient, most holy, wise, good, just, merciful, and so on.

Second, all these confessions define God with the metaphysical categories of essence, nature, substance, or subsistence. Following the ancient formula of Tertullian, they define God as "one divine substance" in three "persons," or "hypostases."

Third, like the Trinitarian tradition they inherited and preserve, all these documents define the triune God almost exclusively in terms of God's *inner being* (the "ontological" Trinity)—in terms of the unity and distinction between a begetting Father, "begotten" Son, and "proceeding" Spirit who are "consubstantial, coeternal, and coequal"

(Second Helvetic Confession, chap. III), or "the same in substance, equal in power and glory" (Westminster Shorter Catechism, Q.6). The definition of the Trinity in these confessions has little or nothing to say about what the Father, Son, and Holy Spirit *do* (the "economic" Trinity)—about the unity and distinction between the "works" of the triune God, later identified as the works of creation and providence, redemption, and sanctification.

This doctrine of the Trinity (and its implications for human life in the world) is subject to four criticisms that contemporary theologians of all traditions have made of Western Trinitarian theology in general:

1. The language is philosophically outdated and no longer makes sense to anyone except academically trained theologians. Ordinary people have to learn to think (or at least to talk) in the categories of ancient Greek philosophy in order to confess the God of Christian faith—an especially strange requirement for non-Western Christians. It is not surprising, then, that while the liturgy of the church is full of Trinitarian language, the doctrine itself is largely ignored as a meaningless "mystery" Christians are supposed to accept, although it has nothing to do with their actual faith and everyday life.

2. Following the classical definition of the Trinity, early Reformed confessions ignore the biblical roots of this doctrine. They certainly intend to speak of the God of the Bible. They can use scripture in a proof-texting way to support their speculative definition of God. They all emphasize that God can be fully known only in Jesus Christ or from the word of God in scripture. But they can define God (even the triune God) without even mentioning the biblical story of God's word and work in the history of Israel and in the life, death, and resurrection of Jesus Christ. Their first thought is not of the living, speaking, acting God of the Bible who is to be loved, trusted, and obeyed; it is rather the thought of a great heavenly Supreme Being who becomes the metaphysical problem of how to put one and three together. (Exceptions to this general rule are the Heidelberg and Calvin's Geneva catechisms, which from the very beginning speak of God from a biblical and christological point of view.)[3]

3. Like classical Western theology in general, early Reformed
confessions presuppose a hierarchical, patriarchal understanding of God and support a similar understanding of human relationships.[4] Their initial definition of God as an absolutely self-sufficient divine monarch, then their definition of
the relation between the members of the Trinity in terms of
begetting, being begotten, and proceeding (even though it is
emphasized that the three are co-equal in power and glory),
both reflect and support what in fact, if not in theory, has always been the most common understanding of God among
Western Christians: God the Father is the number-one, "top"
God who exists as a solitary individual first above the Son and
the Spirit, then above everyone and everything else in creation. This God is related to everything and everyone else as
a God who rules with absolute power, dominion, and control.
"He" is a God unlimited by anyone or anything that could
compromise "his" divine autonomy and freedom to do whatever "he" pleases, a God who maintains divine sovereignty
and freedom by asserting it against all competing claims to
power and freedom. In light of the almost exclusively masculine language with which traditional theology spoke about
God, it is not surprising that many Christians think of God as
the great heavenly *Male* who rules with unlimited power, dominion, and control over everyone and everything else.

Contemporary theologians such as Jürgen Moltmann,
Leonardo Boff, Rosemary Ruether, and Sallie McFague may
exaggerate the influence of the doctrine of the Trinity on the
way people understand themselves and their lives together.
But I find convincing their argument that it has both con-
tributed to and supported some of the most problematic aspects of Western society: extreme individualism, competitive
struggle to achieve and maintain a position of superiority (especially male superiority) over other people, freedom understood as freedom from anyone or anything that limits one's
self-sufficient autonomy, and the exploitation of the natural
world that is understood to be there to be used or misused as
we see fit. Whether or not that was what the classical Christian and Reformed doctrine of the Trinity intended, it has at
least provided theological justification for an individualistic,

hierarchical, and patriarchal understanding of God, God's relation to the world, and human life in it.
4. Although classical Christian and Reformed theology insists on the inseparable unity of Father, Son, and Holy Spirit, it tends in fact to separate them when it comes to speak of what they do as Creator, Redeemer, and Giver of new life. Contemporary theologians are critical especially of two such splits that separate, and even set against each other, the "works" of the one triune God.

I emphasize now this fourth criticism. The first split in the classical doctrine of the Trinity is between the sovereign power of a God who is Creator and Ruler of the world and the love of God in Jesus Christ. A glaring example of this split is the way the Westminster Confession (with much of orthodox Reformed tradition) can define the "eternal decrees" and providence of God only on the basis of speculation about the absolute power of God, who is the "first cause" of all things, without even mentioning what God has done and promises to do in Jesus Christ: "God from all eternity did by the most wise and holy counsel of his own will, freely and unchangeably ordain whatsoever comes to pass" (chap. III.1). "All things come to pass immutably and infallibly" according to "the foreknowledge and decree of God, the first cause" (chap. v.2). We are to understand and accept everything good *and* bad that happens in our individual lives and in the world around us as the will of this all-powerful, immutable God.

Even when classical Christian tradition and early Reformed confessions do come to think about the love of God revealed in Christ rather than the sheer power of God that ordains everything that happens, they think only of the *powerful love* that raised Jesus from the dead, victorious over all the powers of evil, sin, and death. They do not think of God's *self-giving, suffering love* revealed in Jesus' compassion for the sick, his friendship with sinners and outcasts, his defending the cause of the poor and oppressed, and his willingness to suffer and die for such people. According to orthodox Trinitarian theology, Jesus suffered and died only according to his human nature but not according to his divine nature, since by definition a God who is almighty, unchangeable, and "without passions" (Westminster Confession II.1) cannot be touched by or share human weakness, suffering, or death.

Contemporary critics argue that this split between the sovereign power of God *over* us and the love (especially the suffering love) of God *with* and *for* us has become especially intolerable in light of the massive human suffering we have experienced in our time, a time when Christians as well as others ask whether it is possible to believe in a God who is both powerful and loving at the same time. Do we not have to choose between faith in a powerful God who does not care enough to do anything about human suffering and faith in a loving God who is not strong enough to do anything about it—if there is a God?[5]

The second split in classical Trinitarian theology is between the work of God the Father-Creator in the world and the work of God the Son and Holy Spirit in the church.[6] Christian tradition and early Reformed confessions generally assume that while God the Creator rules over all people everywhere with sovereign power, justice, and (sometimes, at least for the "elect") even mercy, the real saving work of God in Christ and the renewing work of God through the Holy Spirit is reserved for Christians in the church. This tendency to divide up the works of the one triune God between what God does inside and outside the Christian sphere has become especially problematic in our religiously pluralistic world, in a time when the question whether and how the triune God of Christian faith is present and at work among the followers of other religious traditions is more pressing than ever.

All the criticisms of the classical Christian and Reformed doctrine of the Trinity we have mentioned add up to the charge that it is neither adequately Christian nor relevant for our time. It is speculatively rather than biblically based. It is linguistically outdated. In our historical social context it is at best irrelevant and at worst dangerous. If we grant that this charge at least raises serious questions about traditional Trinitarian theology, our alternatives are simply to ignore or reject it as some scholars and many ordinary Christians have in fact done, or to reclaim and reinterpret it as contemporary Reformed confessions have begun to do.

The Trinity in
Contemporary Reformed Confessions

We noted earlier that the twentieth century has seen a revival of confession writing in Reformed churches around the world. This revival began with the Barmen Confession of 1934, and so far as I know, with the exception of the Brief Statement of Faith of the Presbyterian Church (U.S.A.) in 1991, all these new confessions were adopted in the '60s, '70s, and early '80s (and therefore do not reflect the most recent theological scholarship). Most of them were strongly influenced by the Trinitarian theology of Karl Barth.[7] With variations, they have several things in common.

First, in contrast with early Reformed confessions, the doctrine of God in contemporary confessions is not grounded in metaphysical speculation about the nature and attributes of God and the relationship between the three Persons in the inner life of the triune God. It is grounded in the word and work of God in the history of Israel and above all in Jesus Christ (thus reclaiming the Christological beginning point that was already there in the Heidelberg Catechism and Calvin's Geneva Catechism).

Second, contemporary Reformed confessions consequently emphasize, as earlier confessions did not, the creative, reconciling, saving, and life-renewing work of the *economic* Trinity—what the living triune God *does*.

Third, contemporary Reformed confessions' biblical-historical understanding of the Person and work of the triune God has led to some new emphases in the Reformed understanding of Christian faith and life: Now God's sovereign power no longer means that God causes everything that happens; it is the loving and just power demonstrated in Jesus Christ—for the benefit of all, not just for the benefit of a chosen few. Now the work of Christ has to do not only with the reconciliation of sinners with God but also with breaking down the barriers of sex, race, class, and nationality that set them against one another. Now the work of the Spirit or of the risen Christ is more than the awakening of faith and new life in Christians and in the church for their own present and future happiness; it is their renewal and empowerment to participate in what the living triune God is doing also outside the church to establish the rule of God's justice and compassion for all people everywhere, for the renewal of all creation.[8]

I believe that all these developments in contemporary Reformed confessions provide a foundation for an understanding of Christian faith and life that is both genuinely biblical and genuinely relevant for our time. But I also believe that if we are to build on that foundation, we have to answer three critical questions that are raised by the Trinitarian theology of early Reformed confessions but which contemporary Reformed confessions so far leave unanswered or half answered.

The Inner Life of the Triune God

How should we think about the relationship between the three Persons of the Trinity in the inner life of God? In the Trinitarian theology of contemporary confessions, all talk about an eternally begetting Father, begotten Son, and proceeding Spirit of the same divine substance has disappeared, but no new language is proposed to take its place. Contemporary confessions speak in a purely functional way of what the three Persons *do* and are typically silent about who they *are* in their interrelationship.

Many Christians in our time like this move from the old metaphysical to a new functional Trinitarianism because thinking of God functionally as Creator, Redeemer, and life-renewing Spirit or Sustainer avoids gender-specific, hierarchical, patriarchal God-talk. But if we do not believe in three Gods, or in one God doing three different things, then we have to say who the one triune God *is* who does these things. If we reject the old hierarchical, patriarchal language and images when we speak of the relationship between Father, Son, and Holy Spirit in the inner life of God (and consequently when we speak of God's relation to the world and human relations in the world), then we must find new and better language and images contemporary Reformed confessions have not yet given us.

The Power and Love of the Triune God

What is the relation between the sovereign power and the suffering love of God? Contemporary Reformed confessions are more biblical than earlier ones in emphasizing that the God of Christian faith is none other than the one we come to know in the history of Israel and in Jesus Christ. But as a rule they still leave unanswered the question early Reformed confessions raise about the relation between the sovereign power of God that raised Jesus from the dead and the self-giving, suffering love of God we see in the life and death of Jesus. This has become an especially important issue in our time, when some theologians and many ordinary Christians think we have to choose between faith in "God the Father Almighty" who rules "from above" to *overcome* human suffering and oppression, and faith in the God we meet in a crucified Lord who is present with and for suffering and oppressed people to *share* their pain and weakness. If we believe in the inseparable unity of the Persons and work of the one triune God, we must find a way contemporary Reformed confessions have not yet shown us to overcome this false alternative.

The Work of God in the World

What is the relation between the presence and work of God among Christians in the church and the presence and work of God among non-Christians outside the church? Contemporary Reformed confessions emphasize more strongly than earlier ones that the life-giving, liberating, reconciling, and life-renewing work of the triune God goes on outside as well as inside the Christian circle, among people of other religions or no religion as well as among Christians. "God is at work beyond our story," as the Declaration of Faith puts it (1.5). But even Reformed Christians who respect what their confessions say about the activity of God in the world beyond the Christian community are unsure whether and how it is possible to confess God's unique revelation and work in Jesus Christ through the Holy Spirit, and at the same time recognize the revelation and work of God among people who do not acknowledge faith in the triune God Christians confess. We must have more help than contemporary Reformed confessions have given us if we are to find a way to be faithful Christians and at the same time to recognize the presence and work of the triune God of Christian faith among people of other religious traditions—and among those who live without any religious faith at all.

I believe that these are the most important questions we have to be able to answer if we are to discern what the living triune God of Christian faith is saying and doing, and what faithful Christians have to say and do, in our pluralistic situation. I also believe that we do not have to invent a new doctrine of the Trinity to deal with these questions. We have only to reclaim and apply more consistently than either earlier or more recent Reformed confessions two ancient guidelines for Trinitarian thinking that contemporary theologians of all traditions have rediscovered. We will identify them now, then in the following chapters see how they help us with some of the specific problems and issues we have discussed in this chapter.

A Trinitarian Theology
for Our Time

The first of the guidelines I have in mind deals with questions raised in both older and more recent Reformed confessions concerning who God *is,* questions about the relationship between the three Persons in the inner being of God, the ontological Trinity. The second guideline deals with questions the confessions raise about what God *does,* questions about the works of the economic Trinity and the relation between these works.

Perichoresis:
The "Social Trinity"

Contemporary theologians in the West (most notably Moltmann and representatives of feminist and liberation theologies)[9] have found in the Eastern Orthodox understanding of the "perichoretic" relationship between the three Persons of the Trinity what I believe is a helpful alternative to the traditional Western hierarchical and patriarchal understanding of this relationship.

The concept of *perichoresis* goes back to the eighth-century Greek theologian John of Damascus. *Peri* (as in perimeter) means "around." *Choresis* means "dancing" (as in the "choreography" of a ballet). Father, Son, and Holy Spirit are like three dancers, holding hands, dancing around together in joyful freedom.

From the perspective of Western monotheism this image of God seems to suggest not one but three personal gods. But *perichoresis* invites us to think in a new way about the meaning of "one" and "personal." The oneness of God is not the oneness of a self-contained individual; it is the unity of a *community* of Persons. And "personal" means by definition *inter*personal: one cannot be truly personal alone, but only in relation to other persons. Such is the unity and personal character of the Father, Son, and Holy Spirit. They are not three independent persons who get together to form a club (or a dance group). *They are what they are* only in relationship with one another. Each *exists* only in this relationship and would not exist apart from it. Father, Son, and Holy Spirit live only in and with and through one another, eternally united in mutual love and shared purpose. Although this understanding of the Trinity as a "social Trinity" may sound suspiciously tritheistic to us Westerners, perhaps it is worth running the risk of being called tritheists when we consider how our understanding both of God and of ourselves changes when we think of the Trinity in a perichoretic way.

Now it is no longer possible to consider thinking of God the Father first of all as a solitary number-one, "top" God, with a begotten Son and proceeding Spirit who are somehow inferior to "him." Now there is no above and below; no first, second, and third in importance; no ruling and controlling and being ruled and controlled; no position of privilege to be maintained over against the other two; no possible rivalry between competing individuals. Now there is only the fellowship and community of equals who share all that they are and have, each living with and for the others in self-giving love, each free not *from* but *for* the other.

It follows that if in God's own deepest inner being God is God-in-community, then that is also what God is in relation to us. The freedom and power of such a God is not freedom and power to do anything God pleases, to dominate and control. It is God's freedom to be with and for us, setting us on our feet and empowering us to be God's faithful covenant partners ("junior partners," to be sure) in God's work in and for the world.

Such an understanding of God would also shape the self-understanding and life together of human beings created in the image of God. If the deity of God is fulfilled in the *community* of Father, Son, and Holy Spirit, then the true humanity of human beings created in God's image is realized only in human community, not in the lonely self-assertion of individuals who seek to be themselves apart from or in competition with other human beings. If in the divine community there is no above and below, superior and inferior, but only the society of equals who are different from one another but live together in mutual respect and self-giving love, so it is also in a truly human society of people who are sexually, racially, socially, politically, and religiously different from one another. If in relation to us God exercises divine power, not to rob us of our human freedom and dignity but to invite and enable us to be partners in God's creative, reconciling, liberating, renewing work in the world, then legitimate human power cannot be used by some (male or female) persons and groups to dominate and control others—it can be used only to free and empower other individuals and groups to work together for the common good of all. A perichoretic understanding of the divine society results in a perichoretic understanding of human society.

There are, of course, problems with this perichoretic doctrine of the Trinity. It does indeed sound tritheistic to those who believe that the Christian religion is one of the great monotheistic religions of the world. Some may be troubled by the fact that it still uses gender-specific language in referring to God as "Father" and "Son," even though hierarchical language to speak of their relationship has been replaced by language of partnership, mutuality, and equality.[10] Others may object that it leads to an understanding of human nature and human society that is at best unrealistic and utopian, and at worst dangerously subversive and un-American. But whatever its limitations, I believe that it enables us to think of God, God's relation to us, and our relation with one another in a new way that is biblically based, authentically Christian, truly Reformed—and desperately needed in our fragmented pluralistic world.

This brings us to a second guideline for Trinitarian thinking.

Indivisible Works
of the One Triune God

The works of the Trinity are indivisible (*Opera trinitatis ad extra indivisa sunt*). This doctrine, which deals with the economic Trinity, originated in the Western Christian tradition. It was emphasized by Augustine in the ancient church, and especially by Karl Barth in the twentieth century. Although it is generally acknowledged as orthodox, in my opinion neither classical nor most contemporary Reformed confessions,[11] nor even recent reinterpretations of the doctrine of the Trinity, have paid enough attention to its importance or thought through its consequences.

Following scripture itself, both ancient and contemporary doctrines of the Trinity assign or attribute different functions, a "division of labor," to the members of the Trinity. The Father is the Creator, Ruler, Protector, and Preserver of the world and all living things in it. The Son is the Judge, Reconciler, and Savior of sinful, needy human beings. The Holy Spirit is God at work in the world to renew and transform the hearts, minds, wills, *and* bodies of individual human beings, and to create new human community where people have been alienated from God and from one another. Three "Persons"—Father, Son, and Holy Spirit. Three works—creation-preservation, reconciliation-salvation, renewal-transformation.

But that does not mean three different Gods, or one God who does three different things. According to scripture there is only *one* God, and *all* of God is involved in *everything* God does.

Creation is not only the work of the Father. It is also the work of the Son: "All things came into being through him" (John 1:3; see also Col. 1:16). And according to Genesis 1:2, creation is also the work of the Spirit (or wind) of God creating order out of chaos.

The work of reconciliation and redemption is the work not only of the Son but of the Father and Spirit too: "*God* was in Christ reconciling the world to himself" (2 Cor. 5:19). It is through the *Spirit* that "we have access to the Father" (Eph. 2:18).

The Spirit's work of "sanctification" that renews us for fellowship with God and other people is also the work of the Father (1 Thess. 5:23) and of the Son (Eph. 5:26).

We may associate different works with one or another of the three Persons, but we cannot separate them. What one wills and does, the other two will and do also. Where one is at work, there the other two are also at work. The purpose and goal of any one are the same as the purpose and goal of the other two. For God the Father, Son, and Holy Spirit are one triune God, and therefore also the *works* of the Trinity are indivisible.

Now at first glance that may look like a safe, harmless statement. But (to paraphrase Karl Barth) it is a bombshell in the playground of Christians. In order to see what radical consequences it has, we have only to look at how it forbids and overcomes the various splits between the person and work of the members of the Trinity that we have seen are explicitly stated, implied, or permitted by both classical and contemporary Reformed confessions, and are still present in the recent work of some theologians of all Christian traditions.

1. If the works of the Trinity cannot be divided, then the sovereign power of "God the Father Almighty" cannot be separated from the self-giving, suffering love of God in Jesus Christ, his only Son our *crucified* Lord—or vice versa. Nor can the church commit itself *either* to a triumphalist ministry that sets out to fix everything that is wrong with the world in the name of the liberating power of God *or* to a passive "ministry of presence" that seeks only to "live in solidarity" with suffering and oppressed people to share their suffering. Our

understanding of both the power and love of God, and our understanding of the task of the church in the world, will be different if we remember that the works of the one triune God cannot be separated or set against each other.

2. If the works of the Trinity are indivisible, then what God the Creator and Ruler of the whole world wills and does *outside* the Christian sphere is not different from what God the Reconciler, Savior, and Lord of Christians wills and does *inside* it. What Christians know about the reconciling, liberating, saving, and renewing work of Jesus Christ in their own lives tells them what the triune God is doing and intends to do in the lives of all people everywhere, including people of other religions or no religion. Our understanding of the task of missions, evangelism, and interreligious dialogue will be different if we remember that the works of the one triune God cannot be separated or set against each other.

3. If the works of the Trinity are indivisible, then the work of the Holy Spirit does not have to do only with the moral, psychological, and spiritual renewal of individual Christians and their fellowship with one another. The Spirit is the Spirit of the God who created, preserves, and defends the life, health, and well-being of all God's creation and all human beings who live in it. The Spirit is the Spirit of the God of Israel, whose presence brings social and political justice for the sake of all who are poor and oppressed. God's Holy Spirit is the Spirit who dwelt in and was promised by Jesus of Nazareth who fed the hungry, healed the sick, befriended sinful outsiders, and loved his enemies. Our understanding of Christian spirituality and spiritual growth will be different if we remember that the works of the one triune God cannot be separated or set against each other.

There are no magic formulas that provide an automatic solution to all the theological, ethical, and social problems that confront us in our pluralistic church and society. But if, as Christians in the Reformed tradition believe, the one fundamental question behind them all is what the living triune God of scripture is saying and doing in our time and place, and what we have to say and do in thankful and obedient response to this living God—then I believe that we are most likely to find God's way and our way in dealing with all the issues that confuse and divide us when we follow these two guidelines for Trinitarian thinking: *perichoresis* and the indivisibility of the works of the Trinity. To this task we now turn in the following chapters.

Chapter Four

Suffering, Liberation, and the Sovereignty of God

The doctrine of the sovereignty of God, especially as it is expressed in the Calvinist–Reformed tradition, is being attacked from all directions today. It is being attacked, for example, by feminist theologians such as Sallie McFague, by Latin American liberation theologians such as Leonardo Boff, and by mainline Protestants such as Douglas John Hall and Jürgen Moltmann.[1] Behind these criticisms lie the old familiar objections that this doctrine robs human beings of both freedom and responsibility and, despite all protest to the contrary, makes God responsible for evil and all the bad things that happen in our individual lives and in the world around us.

But contemporary theologians add a new dimension to this standard objection: the doctrine of the sovereignty of God presupposes a hierarchical, patriarchal understanding of God that provides theological justification for the misuse of human power in familial, social, and political relationships to oppress other people and to rape our natural environment. In the church it produces either pious acceptance of the way things are in the world or an increasingly ridiculous and dangerous "triumphalism" that leads Christians to believe they can "transform" the world to make it conform to their liberal or conservative understanding of the kingdom of God.

If we want a church that is faithful to the gospel and has a reconciling, healing, liberating word to say in our historical and social context, we are told, we must stop thinking of God as "God the Father Almighty," who rules over the world "from above" with absolute power, dominion, and control; who by example supports competition for positions of power, dominion, and control among human beings. We must instead learn to think of a "vulnerable" God who is present *in* and *for* a suffering world as a God of self-giving, suffering love— a God who calls and enables Christians and the church to be present in such a world with the same kind of love to create a truly human society based on mutual care, cooperation, and freely shared responsibility for one another and for the natural world around us.

How should we respond to this widespread attack on a doctrine that has always been close to the center of the Reformed understanding of Christian faith and life? I believe that, first of all, we must confess that the traditional Reformed doctrine of the sovereignty of God is indeed subject to all the earlier and more recent criticisms of it. But I also believe that if we are to be faithful to scripture and formulate a theology relevant for our time, we cannot abandon the traditional Reformed emphasis on God's honor, glory, majesty, and sovereign power. We must learn, rather, to distinguish between two different interpretations of it. The first is the speculative, monotheistic interpretation that Calvin inherited from scholastic medieval theology and that became characteristic of many early Reformed confessions of faith. The second is a Christological, Trinitarian interpretation, which can also be found in Calvin and which was the basis of the "new Calvinism" of Karl Barth and contemporary Reformed confessions influenced by him.[2]

If we can get rid of the old speculative doctrine of the sovereignty of God once and for all, we can make room for a genuinely biblical Christian—*Trinitarian*—understanding of it that is good news both for people who long for a God who cares enough to be present in the depths of their personal and collective suffering to share it, and for people who long for a God who is powerful enough to liberate them from every social, political, and ecclesiastical system that oppresses and dehumanizes.

The Speculative Doctrine of the Sovereignty of God

I begin, then, with the speculative doctrine of the sovereignty of God. I will use Calvin and classical Reformed confessions to illustrate it, but with the understanding that it is only one side of Calvin's

theology and that it is also typical of many Christians today who never
even heard of Calvin or "the Reformed tradition." This understanding of God's sovereignty begins with abstract speculation about the
concept of absolute power as such. It is based on reasoning about what
God would, could, should, and must be and do *if* God is truly sovereign (which of course has always meant what masculine or feminine
individuals and members of a particular race, culture, class, or nation
would be and do if *they* had absolute freedom and power). Calvin and
the early Reformed confessions can buttress this idea of God's sovereignty with copious quotations from scripture, but only to the ne-
glect of other passages that point to a different kind of God. They often use scripture to defend an understanding of God and God's
relation to the world that could just as well be arrived at without any
reference to biblical history at all. This speculative understanding of
the sovereign freedom and power of God has four characteristics,
each of which is echoed in a corresponding understanding of the
meaning of human freedom and power.

Absolute Freedom

The speculative sovereignty of God means that God is arbitrarily free to do anything God pleases. So, for instance, God can decide
either to love or not to love, help or refuse to help, offer forgiveness
or demand punishment in response to human sinfulness, save or
damn. And in fact God demonstrates this sovereign freedom by doing just that: God decides to choose some for well-being and salvation in this life and the next, and to reject, pass over, leave out, and
condemn all the rest. And there we have Calvin's doctrine of election or predestination based on his doctrine of the sovereignty of
God.

South African Reformed theologian John de Gruchy has said in
defense of Calvin that he never confused the elect people of God with
any nation or racial group other than Israel or the church.[3] But once
the idea was accepted that God's freedom is freedom either to include or to exclude, it was inevitable that when the colonial movement began some European and North American Calvinists did take
this step, identifying this or that particular nation or racial or cultural
group as the chosen few and others as those who are left out, passed
over, or rejected. Once it was accepted that God's sovereign freedom

means God's ability to do anything God likes with sinners, it was not too big a step to the idea that those who are sure they are God's elect can do anything they like with any individual or group different from them.

Power That Determines
the Way Things Are

The speculative sovereignty of God means that God wills and determines everything that happens in the world. If God is a sovereign God, "it stands to reason" that nothing can happen against God's will, that everything that happens does so because God ordained and caused it. "Whatever happens in the universe is governed by God's incomprehensible plans" (*Calvin's Institutes of the Christian Religion* I.17.2).[4] "He so regulated all things that nothing takes place without his deliberation" (I.16.3). "Nothing is more absurd than that anything should happen without God's ordaining it" (quoting Augustine, I.16.8). Or in the words of the Westminster Confession (III.1), "God from all eternity did by the most wise and holy counsel of his own will, freely and unchangeably ordain whatsoever comes to pass." So: "If some mothers have full and abundant breasts, but others are almost dry, it is because God wills to feed one more liberally, but another more meagerly" (Institutes I.16.1). "The fruitfulness of one year is a singular blessing of God, and scarcity and famine are God's curse and vengeance" (I.16.5). "Every success is God's blessing, and calamity and adversity his curse" (I.16.8).

That is not all Calvin had to say about God's plans for and work in the world. When he thinks christologically, he can also speak in a very moving and tender way of God's "benevolence," "kindness," and "generosity" toward all God's creatures. But that is not the way Calvin talks when he thinks abstractly about the sovereign power of God. And it is not without good reason that non-Calvinists and ex-Calvinists have always said that despite all protests to the contrary the Calvinist doctrine of the sovereignty of God implies a fatalistic determinism that makes God directly or indirectly responsible for every bad as well as good thing that happens in the world, and demands that pious Christians accept whatever happens to them, their loved ones, and everyone else as the "will of God": health *and* sickness, success *and* failure, life *and* death, good *and* evil.[5]

Dominating and Controlling Power

The speculative sovereignty of God means that God's relation to human beings (and therefore God's will for interhuman relationships) is understood as the relation between dominating control and subservient submission. So, for instance, God has assigned the rich and the poor to their place in the world. The rich are to be grateful for their blessings and the poor are to be "content with their lot and not try to shake off the burden laid upon them by God" (*Institutes* I.16.6). "When we are unjustly wounded by men, let us overlook their wickedness . . . and learn to believe for certain that whatever our enemy has wickedly committed against us was permitted and sent by God's just dispensation" (I.17.8).

Calvin and the classical Reformed tradition could also speak about our responsibility to use the "means" God has provided for us to protect and care for our own and others' welfare. When they thought biblically, they could also say that God ordains the political order to protect the weak and helpless, deliver the oppressed from their oppressors, defend human freedom, and work for the common good of all (IV.20.4). But that is not the way they talk when they think abstractly about the sovereignty of God. And it is no surprise that some Calvinists as well as non-Calvinists (most notably Karl Marx) have argued that the traditional Christian understanding of God's sovereignty demands that the poor and powerless, and victims of injustice, meekly "stay in their place" and accept their helplessness and dependency as the "lot" God has assigned to them.

It is also no surprise that some defenders as well as critics of Calvinism have argued that its understanding of *God's* power as the power to dominate and control leads to the assumption that *human* power is the power of "superiors" to dominate and control "inferiors."

And it is no surprise that both defenders and critics of Calvinism have argued that it encourages ecclesiastical and political authorities to denounce as rebellion against *God* any rebellion against any given oppressive religious, social, or political status quo.

Freedom from
Weakness and Suffering

The speculative sovereignty of God means that God is free from any personal involvement in the weakness, pain, suffering, and death that human creatures experience. In agreement with ancient Greek philosophers and with the main line of Christian tradition both before and after him, Calvin and those who wrote and adopted early Reformed confessions believed that God would not be God if God could be hurt or feel mental or physical pain and anguish, and above all if God could suffer the loneliness and agony of death that is the consequence of human creaturelines and sinfulness. If God is strong, then God cannot be weak. If God is in control, then God cannot fail. If God is above, then God cannot be below. If God is immortal, then God cannot suffer and die.

Of course Calvin and traditional Calvinists believed that God was incarnate in the man Jesus. But in agreement with Christian tradition, they carefully attributed Jesus' weakness, suffering, and death to his human and not his divine nature.[6] The sovereignty of God means by definition God's distance above and absence from everything that is merely human, especially the human experience of suffering and dying. Even when classical Calvinism spoke of God's love, it is love exercised in God's safe, personally uninvolved "condescension" from above, not in identity or solidarity with suffering humanity. The sovereignty of God means that God Almighty can do any and every thing *except* suffer with and for God's suffering creation. God can only look down from the heavenly heights and say, "I love you down there—*if*, of course, you are one of the elect."

Summary

That, then, is "God the Father Almighty" defined by speculative deduction from the concept of sovereign power and freedom as such: a big, powerful God who arbitrarily decides to love, help, and save some people but not others; a God who is responsible for everything good *and* bad that happens to us; a God who rules over us with absolute power and demands from us subservient acceptance of the way things are in our own lives and in the world around us as the "will of God"; a God who is personally untouched and unmoved by human suffering. In Moltmann's language, a great heavenly monarch made in the image of a Roman emperor, a pope, or a medieval king [or queen].[7] This is the God many church people still think they are supposed to believe in if they are faithful Christians—and imitate when they get enough power to do so.

A Trinitarian Doctrine
of the Sovereignty of God

But there is another way to understand the sovereignty of God, a way that Calvin himself and the early Calvinists also knew and that contemporary Reformed theologians such as Karl Barth, Jürgen Moltmann, and Daniel Migliore have rediscovered in our time.[8] According to this way of thinking, the true meaning of God's sovereign power is not discovered by speculating about what God could, would, should, and must be and do if God is really all-powerful. It is not discovered by analyzing our own or others' good or bad experience, then figuring out for ourselves what the will and work of God are that lie behind it. Nor is it discovered by projecting onto God what any of us (male or female, of any race, class, culture, or religious heritage) would be and do if *we* had sovereign power. The real meaning of the sovereignty of God is discovered by listening to what *scripture* tells us about what God actually has said and done and promises to say and do—especially scripture, Calvin himself could say, as it "shows forth Christ" (*Institutes* I.9.3) and leads us to understand also the *power* of God as it is revealed "in Christ alone."[9]

Suppose we took Calvin's "scripture principle" more seriously than Calvin himself and orthodox Calvinists sometimes did. Suppose that when we thought of the sovereignty of God, we thought of the covenant-making, covenant-keeping God whose will for all humanity is made known in the history of little Israel; in the story of the life, death, and resurrection of Jesus Christ; and in the story of the life-renewing Spirit who is the Spirit of the God of Israel and Jesus Christ. Suppose, in other words, we had a *Trinitarian* rather than a speculative monotheistic understanding of the sovereignty of God. And suppose we remembered, following the rules for Trinitarian thinking we looked at earlier, that "God the Father Almighty," "Jesus Christ his only Son our Lord," and the Holy Spirit are inseparably *one* God, first of all in their inner perichoretic community with one another, then in everything they will and do in our individual lives, in the church, and in the world around us. Then all four characteristics of the speculative doctrine of the sovereignty of God I have mentioned would undergo a radical change.

Freedom to Love

God's sovereignty is not God's freedom to do anything God pleases. It is God's freedom always, with everyone, in all things and events, to be the loving and just Lord God is. God *is* love, and God's sovereign freedom is freedom to love — not freedom either to love or not love, to love some people but not others, or sometimes to love and at other times not to love. God's freedom is God's freedom *only* to love, *all* people, *always*. That was the great and perhaps the most important discovery Karl Barth made when he learned that Christian theology is Trinitarian theology.[10]

How do we know that it is true? Because, as we hear over and over again in the Old Testament, God is a God of steadfast love and faithfulness: the God who did indeed "elect" one nation above all others to be God's chosen people, but chose Israel not *instead of* but *for the sake of* all others, to be "a light to the nations" so that the justice of God might reach to the ends of the earth. We know it is true because in the life, death, and resurrection of Jesus Christ, God showed God's love not just for some people but for the whole world. We know it is true because of the promise that the life-giving, life-renewing Spirit of God will be poured out on *all* flesh (Joel 2:28). We know it is true because from all eternity, in the fellowship of Father, Son, and Holy Spirit, in the deepest inner life of God, God *is* love.

That means (contrary to speculative Calvinism) that when we see how plagued by sickness, handicap, poverty, and misery some people are, we have no right to conclude that God must have rejected or "cursed" them. It means that we have no right to conclude, when we see how sinful some people are, or how trapped they are in the consequences of their own or others' sinfulness, that God has given up on them and excluded them from the promises of God's forgiveness, help, renewal, and chance for a fresh start and a new future. The sovereignty of God is not God's freedom to reject and exclude; it is God's freedom to accept and include. It is God's absolutely sovereign freedom to *love*.

Of course, God is also a *just* God, who refuses to let sinful people get by with their sinful rebellion against God and their sinful hostility or indifference toward their fellow human beings. But if the sovereignty of God is God's freedom always, with everyone, to be a loving God, then God's justice cannot be (as Calvin sometimes thought) an *alternative to,* but must be rather an *expression of* God's love. It cannot be the justice of God's curse and vengeance that deals with sinful people by paying them back, getting even, and wiping them out. It can only be justice that confronts, judges, condemns, and sometimes even punishes sinful people for their own good—to help rather than hurt, to restore rather than destroy, to give back the true humanity they have lost in their self-destructive, neighbor-hating, God-rebelling sinfulness. How do we know that is true? Above all, because God's justice is the justice we see executed in the death of Jesus for and not against sinful humanity. It is therefore *loving* justice.

This loving justice of God also tells us what true human justice looks like. Like God's justice, true human justice deals with sinful, lawless individuals and groups by seeking reconciliation rather than retaliation, renewal rather than destruction. (This applies even for guilty sinners who an increasing number of people think should be put to death by capital punishment, for an increasing number of offenses.)

Power That Brings
Hope for the Future

That God is an all-powerful God does not mean that everything that happens is the will of God. It means that God's loving and just will *will* be done. Many things happen that God does not will and does not cause. I believe, for instance, that God does not will or "send" floods, earthquakes, hurricanes, cancer, or babies born with tragic deformities. While the finite and limited creaturely life God wills for us inevitably involves suffering and death in one form or another, at one time or another, I do not believe that God wills or causes the particular way and the particular time they occur—especially when they involve human negligence or indifference in protecting the value and dignity of our own and others' lives. And I am *sure* that God does not will any form of sin, evil, and injustice, or any of the personal and collective suffering that result from them. Sickness, sin, suffering, evil, injustice, and death are by definition what God does *not* will, what God is *against* and is at work to *overcome* and *destroy.*

How do we know that this is true? We know it because God the creator, giver, and preserver of life wills life, not death. We know it because the God of Israel may indeed allow and even will for a time

the individual and collective suffering that is the inevitable consequence of rebellion against God and human lawlessness and injustice,
but remains nevertheless a God of steadfast love and faithfulness who
promises to heal and restore life even to those who do not deserve it.
We know that what we have said is true above all because of what we
learn in the story of Jesus. The rejection of the love and justice of God,
and the rejection of the true humanity, that led to Jesus' death was not
what God willed for the world but precisely what God did *not* will.
And Jesus' resurrection is the manifestation of the sovereign power
of God over all the powers of suffering, evil, injustice, and death. It
means the promise of a new humanity in a new creation which is
surely coming and, by the work of God's Spirit, is already on the
way—a world in which there will be no mourning, or crying, or pain,
or death anymore, anywhere, for anyone.

In light of this Trinitarian hope for the future, faith in the sovereignty of God does not mean pious acceptance of our own or others' suffering and death as the will of God; it means *outrage* and
protest at what a sovereign God of love and justice does not will and
will not tolerate. It does not mean pious acceptance of the way
things are in the world, but hope—and therefore confident work—
for the way things will be when we can say not only in expectant
prayer but in actual experience, "Thine *is* the kingdom and the
power and the glory."

Liberating Power

The sovereign power of God is not power that dominates and
controls. It is power that liberates and enables. The living God of
scripture is not a great heavenly dictator (even a benevolent one) who
demands passive, dependent acquiescence on our part. God rules not
to keep us weak, but to set us on our feet and make us strong, to en-
ergize and empower us freely and gladly to serve God and become in-
struments of God's justice and compassion in the world. God's sovereignty is not the *enemy* but the *source* of human freedom and
responsibility.

It is true that the biblical story is told against a background of the
hierarchical, patriarchal understanding of God that was characteristic
of the ancient world in which it was written and that was still characteristic of Calvin's time. But when we listen to that story as it

actually unfolds, it becomes clear that it is the story of a covenant-making God who willed to be not only *over* but *with* and *for* God's people, a God who delivered them from oppression, went with them on their way, and set them free to become partners in God's work in and for the world. It is the story of a Lord who came not to lord it over others but to serve them, who invited his followers to be not his slaves but his friends, to participate in his work of bringing in the reign of God's love and justice for the good of the whole world. It is the story of the Holy Spirit who is the Spirit of *freedom* (2 Cor. 1:17)—not freedom to be and do anything one pleases, but freedom to love God and neighbor in a community of brothers and sisters in which all the old distinctions between superior and inferior, insiders and outsiders, are abolished, and there is the mutual love and empowerment that is a reflection of the divine community of Father, Son, and Holy Spirit.

Christian life lived by faith in a sovereign God, therefore, does not mean a life of passive receptivity and dependency that sits and waits for whatever God may decide to give us and do for us. It is a life of aggressive Christian discipleship that loves God by loving the world God loves and serves the justice of God that is especially for those who are left out and cannot help themselves. Understanding the legitimate exercise of human power as a reflection of God's exercise of divine power, it is a way of life that uses power in the political sphere and in the church, and in family and in business life, not to dominate and control others (not even by being "nice" to them), but to enable them to become free and responsible human beings who live not just for their own good or the good of others like themselves but for the common good.

Now, whatever criticism may be made of Calvin's and the orthodox Calvinist doctrine of the sovereignty of God, they did sometimes emphasize all the points we have just made. But the next thing that has to be said about a biblical-Trinitarian understanding of the sovereignty of God is something neither Calvin nor the classical Reformed tradition nor any other Christian tradition in the West (except the Lutheran) even imagined. It is an insight first suggested in our time by Karl Barth and then powerfully developed by Jürgen Moltmann. Since then it has been emphasized by many others, most notably Douglas John Hall.[11]

Freedom to Share
Weakness and Suffering

The sovereignty of God is not God's sovereign freedom from and above human weakness, suffering, and dying. It is God's freedom to share the human condition. It is God's power to be not only the great divine helper and savior who dwells in the heavenly heights, but also the friend, companion, and fellow sufferer of suffering human beings "here below." It is God's power to care for people who are victims of their creaturely finitude and vulnerability, and for people who are victims of their own and other's sinfulness, by caring for them not only from a safe distance *above* them but as one who stands in solidarity *with* them. God's sovereignty is God's power to be a God of *self-giving, suffering love* as well as a God of victorious, liberating love.

We have seen that in the history of theology it has always been considered heretical to speak of God's willingness and ability to suffer. But the God we come to know in scripture is not only the God who delivered the people of Israel from slavery and made them a great nation. This is also the God who shared their utter humiliation, powerlessness, and suffering when they were defeated by their enemies and carried off into exile in a foreign land. The God of scripture was present and at work in Jesus of Nazareth not only when he did mighty works of healing and spoke with authority but also when he was rejected as the friend of outcasts and sinners, arrested for treason, and put to death by capital punishment.[12] The God of scripture is the God who comes in the Holy Spirit, not just with problem-solving power but to share the "groaning" of suffering people and a suffering creation that wait in agony for a new creation (Rom. 8:18–23). The sovereign triune God of scripture can also come to us as a weak, *suffering* God—just because, as Moltmann puts it, God is a God of sovereign *love* who can and does care enough to suffer with and for suffering humanity.[13]

To live by faith in *that* kind of sovereign God means to expect and experience the presence and work of God in our own lives and in the world around us when there is pain and sorrow, suffering, and dying, as well as when there is health, happiness, and success; when there are tragic as well as happy endings. Not because God wills and "sends" the bad as well as the good, but because God is so powerful that nothing can happen to us so painful that God cannot be with and for us in the midst of it.

This recognition of the presence and work of a sovereign God of self-giving, suffering love also changes our understanding of what it means to serve God in the world. It requires us to give up the arrogant pretension and terrible burden of thinking that the task of Christians and the church is to love and help all those suffering people "down there" or "out there" from the lofty distance of our superior liberal or conservative virtue, wisdom, and power. It requires us to go to them and stand by them *in* their deserved or undeserved suffering. We are called to do this even when we cannot solve their problems, even when it means risking the hostility and opposition of righteous conservatives or righteous liberals when we make ourselves the friends and advocates of people whom they consider to be the wrong kind of people.

Sovereign Power
and Suffering Love

I believe that one of the most important discoveries of Trinitarian theology in our time is the discovery of the suffering love of the suffering triune God. All cheap and easy talk about a God of sovereign power who is in control of a world in which there is so much poverty, suffering, and injustice is obscene. All self-confident talk about a powerful church that has the mandate and the ability to "transform" society with this or that conservative or liberal social-political agenda, or with this or that evangelistic program, is increasingly absurd in a disintegrating church that cannot solve its own problems, much less the problems of the world. The only gospel that makes sense and can help in what Moltmann calls our "godless and godforsaken" world is the good news of a God who loves enough to suffer with and for a suffering humanity. And the only believable church is one that is willing to bear witness to such a God by its willingness to do the same thing.

But such a gospel, especially as it has caught on and become popular, has its dangers too. Too much talk about the "presence" of God in "solidarity" with suffering people can become a way of hiding a deep skepticism about whether God is powerful enough to *do anything* about their suffering. Pious talk about a "ministry of presence" with those who suffer rightly gives up the arrogant pretension that Christians and the church can fix everything that is wrong in the world, but it can also be an excuse for not doing anything to relieve suffering, restore health, and take an aggressive stand against injustice that causes suffering. People who suffer for one reason or another want more than just "God suffers with you and we Christians do too." They want to know whether there are a God and a people of God who can and will do anything to *help* them. Whether they know it or not, they want to hear about and experience the good news of a Trinitarian God who wills and preserves life, who liberates oppressed people from whatever or whoever oppresses them. They want to hear about and experience a crucified *and risen* Christ who is stronger than the powers of sickness, suffering, sin, and death. They want to hear about and experience the *power* of the Holy Spirit who brings new life where there is death and new beginnings where there are dead ends.

One of the biggest problems in theology today is how we can find our way between a theology of the suffering love of God that offers too little and a theology of the sovereign power of God that promises too much. I believe that the solution lies in thinking through the implications of what we said earlier about faith in the sovereignty of God as *hope for the future* — faith that God's loving and just will *will* be done. That is what it meant both for ancient Israel and for the early Christian community. Most of the time they saw scant evidence of the victorious power of God in their present experience. Little, weak, threatened, and oppressed, like the psalmist and Jesus himself they often experienced only the distance, silence, and absence of God. But even in the depths of their godforsaken weakness and suffering, the people of Israel *remembered* the power of God that delivered them from slavery, and the church *remembered* the power of God that raised Jesus from the dead victorious over the powers of sin and death. Just because of this they confidently *looked forward in hope* to the time when they *would* see and experience the victorious love and power of God in their own lives and in the world around them. In the meantime, as they lived between their *memory* of the sovereign power of God and their *hope* for it, three things happened:

1. They counted on and experienced the comforting and sustaining presence of a God who was there to share their weakness and suffering.

2. Now and then, here and there, once in a while, even in the present, they experienced what Barth calls little, provisional, temporary but real evidences of the liberating power of God at work in their lives and in the world: a few lives saved and restored to health where only death had reigned, a little more justice where there had been only massive injustice, moments of reconciliation where there had been only hostile alienation—little signs that their memory and hope were not in vain and that there was more to come.[14]

3. And that gave them the confidence and courage, despite all opposition, setbacks, failures, and defeats, to keep up an active struggle for the wholeness, justice, freedom, and peace of the kingdom of God they were sure was already on the way and would surely come—not because of what *they* might be able to accomplish but because of what the *sovereign God* in whom they believed could and promised to accomplish with or without their puny little help.[15]

That is what it means to be Christians and a Christian church in our time too. Dependence on and witness to the self-giving, suffering love of God for suffering people in a suffering world? Yes! But also the certainty that we and all people everywhere come from and go to meet a life-giving, liberating, reconciling, life-renewing triune God of sovereign power who is not only "present" but present and *at work* (and who invites *God's people* to be not only present but present and at work), moving toward the new humanity in a new heaven and earth that are on the way and will surely come.

We have to talk about the sovereignty of God in a way quite different from that of Calvin and the classical Reformed tradition. But after we have corrected everything that is wrong with them from the point of view of our superior wisdom and understanding, we might just discover that Calvin was dead right after all when he said that to believe in the sovereign power of God means "gratitude for the favorable outcome of things, patience in adversity and also incredible freedom from worry about the future" (*Institutes* I.17.7).

Chapter Five

Jesus Christ
and the
Religions of the World

"No one knows the Father except the Son and anyone to whom the Son chooses to reveal him" (Matt. 11:27). "There is salvation in no one else, for there is no other name under heaven given among mortals by which we must be saved" (Acts 4:12). "I am the way, and the truth, and the life. No one comes to the Father except through me" (John 14:6).

What should Christians who live in today's religiously pluralistic world do with such texts? Christians have always known, of course, that they live in a world in which there are many "so-called gods," and they have always confessed that "for us there is one God, the Father, from whom are all things and for whom we exist, and one Lord, Jesus Christ, through whom are all things and through whom we exist" (1 Cor. 8:5–6). They have always known that their confession of the uniqueness of God's self-revelation and saving work in Jesus of Nazareth raises questions about the relation between Christians and the followers of "other religions." But the church's response to the problem of religious pluralism has varied in the course of its history.

For the first three centuries, Christians were members of a powerless, despised, and often persecuted religious minority. For them, religious pluralism meant the challenge to remain faithful to the God revealed in Jesus Christ, willing to pay the cost of refusing to acknowledge or serve any of the gods that were tolerated or officially recognized in the world around them.

Everything changed in the fourth century when (at least partly for political reasons) the Roman emperor Constantine became a Christian and made Christianity the one legal religion of the empire. All Europe became automatically "Christian" almost overnight. Christians were no longer a threatened religious minority; now they were the powerful religious majority. For centuries after that European and, later, North American Christians assumed that the followers of other religions lived either "over there" in other parts of the world or as a minority in the "Christian West." They took it for granted that the church's task (often with the support of this or that government and/or business enterprise) was to work for the voluntary or forcibly imposed conversion of these "outsiders" to Christianity, the one true religion. They often took it for granted also that if non-Christians invaded "Christian territory" from without or challenged the rule of the Christian majority from within, they were to be silenced, marginalized, excluded, and perhaps even killed. Once persecuted, Christians sometimes became persecutors themselves.

For the past two hundred years it has become increasingly clear that the "Constantinian era" is coming to an end. It is no longer possible (if it ever was) to speak realistically of the "Christian West" or "Christian America." Many people in Europe and North America live without any serious religious commitment at all, or with commitment to vague general "moral principles" and "religious values" without any specific Christian content. Followers of "other religions" who once lived somewhere else are now our fellow workers and next-door neighbors, in some places outnumbering Christians. (There are, for instance, more Muslims than Presbyterians in the United States today.) Even where Christians are in the majority, most Western countries, in principle at least, grant people the freedom to practice whatever religion they please (or no religion at all)—without preferential treatment being given to the beliefs, values, and practices of any one religious group, and without the members of any religious (or nonreligious) minority being excluded or discriminated against in governmental policy and public assemblies.

Especially when we look with a global perspective beyond Western nations, it is clear that we live in a world in which the Christian religion is only one of several great world religions, and that Christians are and may remain the minority they were at the beginning. It is also increasingly clear that there can be no peace within or among nations anywhere unless there is peace among followers of different religious traditions. We live in a world, in other words, in which tolerant, open "interreligious dialogue" has become a necessity, not just something a few liberals like to talk about.

Can or should Christians (including Christians in the Reformed tradition) who live in such a "post-Constantinian," "post-Christian," religiously pluralistic world still confess that Jesus is *the* way, *the* truth, and *the* life, in whom *alone* salvation is found? That is the question we will consider here, looking especially at its implications for the relationship between Christians and followers of other religious traditions. Since we live in a pluralistic church, however, in which Christians themselves do not agree in their answer to the question, we must also consider to some extent the need for "interreligious dialogue" *within* the Christian community.

Beginning at the Center

It has become customary to say that Christians have some variation of three major alternatives in dealing with non-Christians and with other Christians who are different from them: exclusivism, pluralism, or inclusivism.[1]

1. *Exclusivism.* This is the traditional Christian position. Jesus Christ is *the* way, *the* truth, and *the* life. There is no other name, no other way, no other truth. That means that, whether in a gentle and loving way or flat out, Christians have to say to non-Christians: "The Christian religion (or our church's particular version of it) is the one true religion, and all others are false. We have the truth and you don't. We worship and serve the one true God; you worship and serve false gods. Our way of life is right, and yours is wrong. We live in the light; you grope in darkness. God is for us, and we are and will be saved; God is against you, and you are and will be damned unless you too accept Jesus Christ as your Lord and Savior, become a Christian, and join the (or our) church. Only then will you know the real truth about God and

yourself, find true happiness, know how to live rightly in this life, and have any hope for salvation when you die."

2. *Pluralism.* This is a modern alternative to traditional Christian exclusivism. *For us Christians,* Jesus is the way, the truth and the life. But there are also other paths to God, other expressions of the truth about God and human life, other ways to live a good and meaningful life. *We Christians* have experienced the enlightening, renewing and saving presence and work of God in Christ, but *others* may find the same thing in other religious figures. Jesus is *one* way, but not the *only* way. There is no other name by which *we Christians* are saved, but there *are* other names by which others are saved. Indeed, beneath all the historical, cultural, and ritual differences that distinguish the great religions of the world, we can discover a common faith in one God who through a universal divine *logos* or spirit is savingly present and at work in them all.

Pluralists generally emphasize that this acknowledgment of religious and ethical truth in other religious traditions does not mean a kind of wide-open relativism that says that all religions are equally true. There may be some religions (including some versions of Christianity) that are superstitious, personally destructive, and socially and politically oppressive. But wherever we encounter a religion that acknowledges the mystery of a loving and just transcendent Reality that gives direction and meaning to human life, promotes psychological wholeness, maintains high ethical standards, contributes to the liberation of all people, and integrates individual persons and nations into a larger human community—there we may recognize a true, valid, and saving religion, even though its followers may call on the name of Muhammad, Moses, the Buddha, or some other name instead of the name of Jesus.[2]

3. *Inclusivism.* A third alternative is a mediating position between exclusivism and pluralism often identified with Karl Rahner's idea of "anonymous Christians."[3] With exclusivists, this position argues that Christianity is the true, unique, and definitive religion. But with pluralists, it insists that God's grace is also at work outside the Christian circle, en-

abling non-Christians also to be genuinely religious, ethically responsible "Christianlike" people even though they do not know and confess Jesus Christ as Lord and Savior. Therefore not only confessing Christians but also those who live in the light of the best and most authentic religious faith that is available to them will be saved, for in their own way they are Christians too.

I believe that we must reject all three of these alternatives because they force us finally to choose between two unacceptable positions: *either* (with the exclusivists) we must choose to be faithfully Christian at the expense of being arrogant and intolerant of other religions; *or* (with the pluralists and inclusivists) we must choose to be open and tolerant of religious differences at the expense of compromising the unique claims and promises of the Christian gospel. Those of us who are unhappy with both choices seek a way of understanding Christian faith and life that is faithfully Christian and *at the same time* open to the truth that is found in religious commitments other than our own.

The usual way of trying to do this is to look for a way to combine the strengths of the exclusivist, pluralist, and inclusivist positions. But I believe that the way to achieve the goal is first to recognize a *weakness* they all share, then seek a genuinely new fourth alternative.

Their common weakness is that in one way or another all of them tend to lose sight of the Person who stands at the center of Christian faith and life. *Exclusivists* tend to be more interested in the superior wisdom, virtue, and privilege of Christians, Christianity, or the Christian church than in Jesus Christ himself. *Pluralists* tend to be less interested in what the gospel tells us about Jesus than in measuring the truth of the Christian religion and all other religions by their own philosophical, psychological, ethical, or ideological criteria for establishing what any true religion must look like. *Inclusivists,* in my opinion, are correct in their concern to acknowledge the free grace of God that is at work wherever and however God chooses. But they tend finally to make knowledge of the truth and grace of God *in Jesus Christ* unnecessary — though they may sometimes suggest that the (or a particular) *church's understanding* of that truth and grace is the standard by which claims to truth and goodness in other religious traditions are validated or invalidated.

I believe (and this is my proposed fourth alternative) that if we want to understand Christian faith and life in a way that is authentically Christian and at the same time be open to listen to and learn from other religious perspectives, we must begin with the Christian confession that seems at first glance to make honest and fruitful interreligious conversation most difficult. We must begin precisely with the confession that *Jesus Christ* is the way, the truth, and the life.

But if that confession is to open rather than close the door to such a conversation, we must first make a clear distinction between the gospel of Jesus Christ and the Christian religion (or any church's understanding of it), then ask afresh who this Jesus is whom Christians confess.

The Christian gospel
and the Christian Religion

In the last full volume of the *Church Dogmatics* Karl Barth wrote: "The statement that Jesus Christ is the one Word of God has nothing to do with the arbitrary exaltation and glorification of the Christian in relation to other people, of the church in relation to other institutions, or of Christianity in relation to other conceptions."[4] I believe that Barth is right: to be a Christian is to exalt and glorify Jesus Christ, not Christianity in general or the Christianity of any particular church. It is to believe that what is good and true is not defined by what *we Christians* are, what *we* know, and what *we* have to offer to others. It is defined rather by who *Jesus* is, the truth *he* brings, and what *he* has to offer. We Christians and our church are not called and empowered to instruct, judge, reconcile, liberate, transform, and save the world; that is *his* work. It is the good news of Jesus Christ, not the superiority of Christians, their church, or their religion that we have to proclaim in word and deed to the world.

The problem, of course, is that we never have the pure gospel of Christ to proclaim. In the words of the Confession of 1967, "The Christian religion, as distinct from God's revelation of himself, has been shaped throughout its history by the cultural forms of its environment."[5] For centuries it was shaped by the language, philosophical categories, political options, and cultural patterns of Greco-Roman civilization. More recently it has been interpreted through the lens of the presuppositions and questions of the eighteenth-century

Enlightenment. Ancient or modern, it has traditionally been representatives of the "Christian West" or "Christian North America" who have defined the gospel and who sponsored and exported it around the world. Protesting against the Western monopoly on the gospel, Christians in Latin America, Africa, and Asia now define it from the perspective of *their* cultural contexts. "Postmodern" Christians everywhere do the same from the perspective of their particular racial group, social class, or sexual identity and orientation. What "the gospel" is depends to a great extent on who is defining it, in which context, and for or against whose self-interest.

The contextual relativity of these different interpretations of the gospel is not bad in itself. On the contrary, it is a sign of commitment to communicate the gospel in understandable and relevant ways in every new time, place, and situation. But, as especially theology in the Reformed tradition has always insisted, it is always a perversion of the gospel to identify or confuse it with any particular interpretation of it. When that happens, it is no longer the gospel of Jesus Christ that is proclaimed and defended, but the culturally and historically conditioned self-understanding of some individual or group in the church.

And the results are always the same. First, those who are sure that their interpretation of the gospel is the correct one try to "help" others understand and accept their true religion, true morality, true vision of a just political and social order. If that does not work, then in one form or another, violent or nonviolent, come the crusades, inquisitions, religious wars, and colonial or economic or cultural imperialism that try to *force* everyone to accept and live by this or that version of true Christianity. All in the name of the Christian gospel, of course. But the gospel in the service of Western individualism, capitalism, and the political and economic power of this or that Christian nation—or more recently the gospel in the service of Marxist socialism or this or that version of "political correctness." (We ought not to be overly cynical about this. Once in a while, here and there, Christians and the church have said and done a few *good* things in the name of Jesus Christ. But the danger is always there as soon as the gospel is made subservient to anyone's version of true Christianity.)

Is there anything we can do to free the gospel from its cooption and perversion by various forms of what Barth called a self-exalting or self-glorifying Christianity that makes Christians and their particular version of the gospel superior not only to other people but to Christ himself?

The most popular response in our time is to begin immediately talking about "dialogue"—first between fellow Christians who are different from each other, then with representatives of other religious traditions. But, indispensable as it is, interreligious dialogue is not enough. It can help us see as we can never see by ourselves how we all confuse the gospel with our own personal, ideological, and cultural biases and presuppositions. But it cannot tell us what the gospel itself is. It can help us to listen to and learn from what others tell us about who they are and what they believe. But it does not help us know what we have to say to them about who *we* are and what our faith teaches *us* to believe.

I believe that if we really want to distinguish between the authentic Christian gospel and the various forms of Christian religion that in one way or another are always a distortion of it, and if we want to hold up our end of a mutually informative and helpful interreligious dialogue with others, we must first turn for help not to interreligious conversation itself but to the radical claims of the Christian gospel about Jesus Christ. For it is not "dialogue" but *he* that is the way, the truth, and the life. Christ himself—not the true Christianity of any one church or group in the church, traditional or contemporary, conservative or liberal, male or female, of any race or class or culture. Jesus Christ alone—not the religious and ethical insights of Jews, Muslims, and Buddhists *or* Christians, nor even what they may discover they have in common if they work at it hard enough. For there is no other name by which we can be saved.

Now of course the name "Jesus Christ" is not a magic key that opens all doors. We have just confessed that it can be used to justify the very arrogant and intolerant exclusivism that is a denial of the gospel and cuts off interreligious dialogue. Every church or group within the church can and often has made Jesus in its own image and used his name to serve its own self-glorifying and self-serving version of the gospel, and to discredit everyone else's.

But what would happen if we stopped using the gospel's claim that Jesus is the way, the truth, and the life to glorify and exalt us Christians or any particular version of true Christianity? What if we heard it first of all as an invitation to ask afresh who *he* is and what *he* says and does, not to congratulate ourselves on what *we* are and what *we* have to say and do? And what if we looked for the answer in the church's ancient confession of Christ in the context of its confession of the *triune God* to whom scripture bears witness—the one God whose works of creation, liberation, reconciliation, redemption, and life renewal are never separated? I believe *then* we would be in a position to discover an understanding of Christian faith and life that is uniquely and faithfully Christian and at the same time open to a genuinely productive and mutually corrective conversation with fellow Christians who are different from us, as well as with followers of other religious traditions—*just because* we believe that Jesus Christ is the way, the truth, and the life.

The Way, the Truth, and the Life

Who then is this Jesus whom Christians confess to be the way, the truth, and the life, in whose name alone salvation is found?

The Work of God the Creator

Jesus is one in whom is revealed the will and work of the God who is the Creator and Ruler of heaven and earth, the Giver, Protector, and Defender of the life, health, and well-being of all creatures everywhere. He is the self-revelation of the God whom Israel confessed before there were any Christians, the God who from the beginning ordained that there should be political leaders and civil governments in the world to preserve freedom and justice in human society, defend the weak, deliver the oppressed from their oppressors, provide for the safety and promote the common good of all people.[6] To confess the unique self-revelation of God in Jesus Christ, then, is to confess not just what God has done, is doing, and promises to do for and among us Christians; it is to recognize what the life-giving, life-preserving Creator of the world has been doing, is doing, and intends to do also outside the Christian circle, among all people everywhere, including those who do not know, confess, and voluntarily serve Jesus Christ as their Lord.

The Work of God
the Reconciler and Redeemer

Who is the one whom Christians confess to be the way, the truth, and the life? According to the New Testament, he is the expression of

God's love not just for Christian believers but for all humanity, the one in whom God was at work to reconcile *the whole world* to himself. He came not to give his followers everything they wanted to be happy, successful, and secure now and forever, but to announce and usher in the worldwide reign of God's justice and compassion for *everyone.* He was the friend not just of law-abiding, God-fearing insiders, but of sinful, unbelieving, or different-believing outsiders. He believed that caring for suffering and needy human beings was more important than conformity to the moral and theological requirements of religious orthodoxy. He came not to condemn, defeat, and lord it over those who rejected him but to give his life for them, to restore to them their own true humanity and to reconcile them to God and their fellow human beings. And God raised *him* from the dead and made *him* to be the crucified and risen Lord over all principalities and authorities everywhere—not just Lord over the church or Lord in the hearts of Christians, but risen Lord who continues his healing, reconciling, liberating, saving work everywhere in the world. Even where he is not yet known, acknowledged, and served; even before Christians get there to tell others about him.

The Work of God
the Renewer of Life

Who is the one who is the way, the truth, and the life? He is the one who was empowered by the Spirit of the God of Israel, the Spirit who from the very beginning has been the origin of all life, beauty, truth, goodness, and freedom *wherever* it appears.[7] He is the one who said that the same life-giving, life-renewing, community-creating Spirit who dwelt in him, and whom he promised to his followers, is a spirit that "blows where it wills," a Spirit not trapped in or possessed by Christians and their church but is loose in the world to create not only new Christians but a whole new humanity.[8]

The Work of the One Triune God

In short, Jesus Christ is the way, the truth, and the life of the triune God who is not only present and at work among and for the sake of Christians but present and at work among and for the sake of all people everywhere—including people of other religious faiths, people of no religious faith, and, who knows, maybe even fellow Christians for whom we have contempt because they are too liberal, too conservative, or too pietistic in what they believe and too tradition-bound or tradition-shattering in the way they live.

Where then shall we begin interreligious dialogue with people whose faith and life are different from our own? I believe that Lesslie Newbigin has it right: "We must begin with the great reality made known to us in Jesus Christ, that God—the creator and sustainer of all that exists—is in his own triune being an ocean of infinite love overflowing to all his works in all creation and to all human beings."[9]

Consequences for Interreligious Dialogue

Now what are the implications of faith in such a Christ, and therefore in such a triune God, for Christians' encounter with people who are outside the Christian circle altogether, or outside their particular circle of Christians? I mention two. The first has to do with Christian openness to mutually informative and corrective conversation, the second with what evangelical theologian Clark Pinnock calls "a strategy for *truth-seeking* encounters in interreligious dialogue."[10]

Openness

In the first place, if we remember who Jesus and the triune God revealed in him are, we cannot look at people of other faiths or different understandings of the Christian faith as our enemies and the enemies of our God. We can only recognize them as fellow human beings who just like us are created in the image of God;[11] people who just like us are loved and cared for by God; people for whom just as for us Christ lived, died, and rose again; people who just like us are promised the life-renewing Spirit of God.

Moreover, if we know that when we go to meet such people, we do not go into foreign territory but into territory where the living triune God has already been at work before we get there, we will expect and gladly welcome evidence that the grace and truth we have come to know in Jesus Christ have reached into their lives too. We will *expect* and *be glad* to hear them say things about their God and their faith that sound remarkably similar to what we have to say about our God and our faith. Without the slightest trace of reluctance or suspicion, we will thankfully welcome such similarities as confirmation of our own faith in a gracious God who is present and at work not only among us but everywhere in the world.

More than that, we will be prepared to discover among those whose faith and life are different from ours a depth of faith, personal integrity, gratitude for the goodness of God, and self-giving love for others that put us Christians to shame. We sometimes see in them more of the way, the truth, and the life taught and demonstrated by Jesus than we see in our own lives and in the Christian community. Those "outsiders" (whom Jesus called "the last") may sometimes teach us (who consider ourselves "the first") what our own faith looks like when it is actually practiced, and remind us that *we* need to repent and be born again as much as they do.

Just when we are committed to the way, the truth, and the life of the triune God revealed in Jesus Christ, in other words, we will enter into dialogue with people whose faith is different from our own not only because of what we have to offer them, but because of what they have to offer us. Quoting Max Warren (whose language is still unfortunately sexist), Clark Pinnock puts it this way:

> We remember that God has not left himself without witness in any nation at any time. When we approach the man of a faith other than our own, it will be in a spirit of expectancy to find how God has been speaking to him and what new understanding of the grace and love of God we may ourselves discover in this encounter. Our first task in approaching another people, another culture, another religion, is to take off our shoes, for the place we are approaching is holy. Else we may find ourselves treading on men's dreams. More seriously still, we may forget that God was here before our arrival.[12]

Now all such talk about wide-open Christian readiness to be instructed and corrected by conversation with people of other faiths (or different versions of Christian faith) immediately raises Pinnock's question about *truth-seeking* encounters. This leads me to a second implication of Trinitarian Christian faith for Christian participation in interreligious dialogue.

Truth-Seeking Encounters

How can we *recognize* the grace and truth of the triune God when we run into it in interreligious conversation? By what *norm* can we distinguish between what is true and what is false, what is faithful to the gospel and what compromises it for the sake of a lowest-common-denominator religion that ignores or glosses over real differences? My answer (not exactly the same as Pinnock's) is that the norm is the same commitment to Jesus Christ as the way, the truth, and the life that leads us to dialogues in the first place.

Does that mean we can make the arrogant claim that we Christians are right after all and that we will accept from others only that which confirms what we already know and believe? Is not such a claim the end of a real two-way dialogue in which both sides have something to learn from the other? No, it means rather that the grace and truth of the triune God we come to know in Christ is the standard by which *all* religions, *including our own,* are judged, corrected, and set free to know, love, and serve the one true God who is not the captive of *any* religion. It means, in the words of the Confession of 1967, that "the reconciling word of the gospel is God's judgment upon *all* forms of religion, including the Christian" (*Book of Confessions* 9.42, emphasis added). What Lesslie Newbigen says about the relation between the Christian gospel and culture in general is also applicable here: "To affirm the unique decisiveness of God's action in Jesus Christ is not ar rogance; it is the enduring bulwark against the arrogance of every culture [or religion] to be itself the criterion by which others are judged."[13] The grace and truth of the triune God revealed in Christ is not a weapon to use against those whose faith and life are different from our own in order to prove our superiority over them. It is the norm for truth-seeking encounters that enables us to appreciate what is good and true in the practice of their religion and at the same time to criticize what is not good and true in the practice of our own religion.

Four examples will show how this Trinitarian norm for interreligious dialogue works.

Respect for
Physical-Material Life

We may gratefully recognize the presence and work of the God whom Christians confess to be the world's Creator and Preserver wherever people anywhere (Christians or not) treat physical-material life with respect and deal with it responsibly. This includes the physical-material life of animals as well as human beings, and that of life-giving land, plants, water, and air.

On the other hand, wherever people anywhere (including people who call themselves Christians) are indifferent to or show contempt for the physical-material life and health of any part of the created world—or when they exploit and destroy its natural resources for the wealth, comfort, and power of some at the expense of others—there is exposed lack of faith in, indeed opposition to, the God our own faith tells us is the God who created the world and called it good.

In our time, it is equally important to add that wherever people anywhere (including people who call themselves Christians) *worship* any part of the created world, there we see only blasphemy against the Creator and the worship of false gods. An example is the romantic worship of nature and natural forces instead of their Creator. We see it also when human beings convince themselves that they worship and serve God when they actually worship and serve only the health and beauty of their own bodies, their rationality and intelligence, or their male or female sexuality.

The Value and Dignity
of Human Life

We may gratefully recognize the presence and work of the Creator in whom Christians believe wherever people anywhere (including people whose religion is different from our own) respect and protect the dignity and value especially of *human* life, both in personal relationships and in public policy. This includes *every* human life, female *and* male, of every race, class, and culture; friends *and* enemies; those we consider worthy, deserving, and productive *and* those whom we consider worthless, undeserving, and useless.

On the other hand, wherever people anywhere (including those who call themselves Christians) are indifferent to or hold contempt for any human life, however sinful or threatening to their own personal or collective security and self-interest—there the God Christians confess is absent or present only in judgment. For, as Paul Lehmann once put it, the God of Christians is the God who became a human being, for the sake of human beings, to make and keep *all* human life human.[14]

Authentic Religion and Morality

We may recognize the presence and work of the God who Christians believe was uniquely revealed in Jesus Christ wherever and among whomever (including Jews, Muslims, Hindus, and followers of other religions) we see Jesus' kind of religion and morality: There those whom the rich and powerful ignore or reject are befriended. Those whom the (liberal or conservative) pious and good exclude are invited in. Love is offered without any qualifications about what people must be or believe or do in order to be eligible for it. Justice is administered to reconcile, heal, help, and restore rather than to pay back, get even, punish, and destroy. Religious faith and morality are motivated by love for God and fellow human beings rather than by self-serving desire to be rewarded for believing and doing the right things, or to escape punishment for not doing so. Whenever and among whomever (whether they are Christians or not) we see that kind of faith and life, there Christians gladly recognize the presence and work of the God they have come to know in the life, death, and resurrection of Jesus Christ.

On the other hand, wherever people (also those who claim to be Christians) do *not* exhibit that kind of religion and morality, there we must say that the God Christians confess is not yet known at all, or has been forgotten or rejected.

Freedom for
a New Humanity

Finally, we may gratefully recognize the presence and work of the Spirit of the triune God in whom Christians believe wherever and among whomever (including non-Christians) people are being set free from everything that enslaves and dehumanizes them. Where the Spirit of God is, there is *freedom*: There is freedom from the fears and animosities that set family members and people of different genders, races, classes, and religions against one another. There is freedom from self-destructive addictions, whether addiction to alcohol and drugs or addiction to narcissistic preoccupation with one's own health, happiness, and the accumulation of power and possessions in this life and eternal salvation in the next. There is freedom from the paralyzing despair or apathetic resignation that comes with the conviction that nothing can ever be different in one's own life or in the world. There is freedom *for* new beginnings in personal and social relationships, and hope for what the life-renewing Spirit of God can and will do in a world that was, is, and will be the world of a just and compassionate God.

On the other hand, wherever any people anywhere (including people who congratulate themselves for being Christians) fearfully, hopelessly, defensively, or (worst of all) *piously* accept the way things are; where there is resistance to every attempt to create a more just and compassionate human community because of a cynical "hermeneutics of suspicion" that assumes that human relationships are *always, only* motivated by self-interested power struggles; where there is the pious argument that God has ordained some people to be healthy and some sick, some rich and some poor, some superior and some inferior, some included and others excluded—wherever and among whomever that is going on, there the Spirit of the living God Christians confess is resisted or not believed in at all. For where the life-renewing Spirit of God is at work, there people are set free to move toward a *new* humanity in a *new* world.

The purpose of serious interreligious conversation between people of different religious commitments is more than just to give each other the opportunity to share religious experience and convictions. It is more than just to enable people to understand each other better, be more tolerant of each other, and live together in peace. It is to discern the *truth* about God and the will of God for our lives. But the truth we Christians seek to discern in such dialogue is not *our* truth. It is *God's* truth, the truth of the triune God revealed in Jesus Christ. It is truth that exposes, judges, condemns, and corrects the limitations, fallibility, and sinfulness of us Christians and our Christianity as well as those of other people and their religion. More important than that, it is also truth about what Pinnock calls the "boundless generosity" of the triune God who is present and at work in the world for and among "them" as well as "us."[15]

If we want to discern and be faithful to that truth, we will enter into conversation with people whose faith is different from our own (both outside and inside the Christian community) with honest recognition of the differences that separate us; with great modesty about our own piety, wisdom, and virtue; and with eager willingness to meet our own God in our conversations with them. And we will do it with a boundless generosity of our own that is the very best witness we could possibly make to the crucified and risen Lord who is the way, the truth, and the life.

Chapter Six

Worldly Spirituality

It is often taken for granted that our pluralistic society is an ever-increasingly secular society. The news media scarcely even mention religion except when there is a juicy sex or financial scandal among the clergy. Or when some weird sect prepares for the end of the world. Or when the right-wing Christian minority tries to impose its understanding of Christian faith and life on public schools and governmental policy. Or when wars break out between hostile religious groups in other parts of the world. Ordinarily, it is assumed, we live in a consumer-oriented, pleasure-seeking society that does not even bother to reject religious belief but simply ignores it as irrelevant more often than not *comically* irrelevant, as when a typically harmless, blundering minister, priest, or rabbi appears on the movie or TV screen.

But that assumption of a rampant secularism is called into question by the fact that there is a widespread hunger in our society for a "new spirituality" or "spiritual renewal" both inside and outside established religious communities. Outside them it is expressed in the popularity of the New Age movement, in movies about people who return from the dead to straighten things out on earth, and in the appearance of angels on the cover of *Time* magazine. Among Christians it is expressed in the continuing growth of pentecostal and charismatic movements in mainline churches as well as in "off-brand"

Christian sects, and in the popular demand (even in seminaries) for literature and study groups on "spiritual development."

It is not hard to identify the roots of this spiritual hunger. However differently church people and outsiders seek to satisfy it, they all talk about it in the same way. They feel oppressive boredom, meaninglessness, stagnation, burnout, hopelessness, *deadness* in their individual lives and personal relationships, in their work (even in "good works" for justice and peace), in the political and social structures that shape their lives — and in churches that conduct business as usual (or have nothing to talk about except sex) when the world is falling apart around them. These people hunger for new freedom, joy, enthusiasm, and energy that will make them "feel alive" again and enable them to hope that things can be different in their own lives and in the world around them. Their hunger for a new spirituality is hunger for new life in the midst of all the deadness in and around them. Whatever words they use to talk about it, they hunger for the one whom Christians know as the Holy Spirit, the Lord and Giver of new life.

A church that is faithfully Christian and genuinely relevant, then, must deal with this strange hunger for the Spirit of God that persists under the surface of our secular society as well as in the churches themselves.

The problem, of course, is that different people (including Christians) have different ideas about what true spirituality is and about what or who the life-giving spiritual power is that makes it possible. One reason for these differences is that all of us, Christians and non-Christians alike, tend to confuse the inner guidance of the Spirit with our own deepest feelings and thoughts, and the empowerment of the Spirit with the fulfillment of our personal desires and ambitions and those of others like us in gender, race, class, and political conviction. So, for instance, church members are not always wrong in suspecting that their leaders sometimes piously claim to be "led by the Spirit" when in fact they are only defending their own personal or collective self-interest and conservative or liberal ideological biases. And some church leaders are not always wrong in suspecting that church members and outsiders are doing the same thing when they complain that the church is not "spiritual" enough and does not meet their "spiritual needs."

There is another reason, however, for our differences in discerning the presence and work of the Spirit. The Spirit of God is not the only spirit at work in and among us. There are other spirits too: the spirit of the times, the spirit of capitalism or Marxism, the spirit of narcissism, and the spirits of envy, revenge, malice, greed, lust for power, and other evil spirits that are as active in the church as anywhere else.

If we want to distinguish between a true spirituality that fulfills people's spiritual hunger and a false spirituality that is bound to lead to self-deception and disappointment, we must learn to "test the spirits to see whether they are from God" (1 John 4:1). And Christians believe that the way to do that is to test everything we think we know about the Spirit's presence and work in our own lives and in the world around us by what the Bible tells us about who the Spirit is: the Spirit of the God of Israel, the Spirit who was uniquely present and at work in Jesus of Nazareth, the Spirit of the risen Christ who continues to be present and at work throughout the world but is recognized and confessed in the community gathered and sent out in his name.

In other words *the Christian doctrine of the Trinity* is the clue to discerning who the Holy Spirit is in distinction from all the false spirits in and around us. That ought to be obvious enough for Christians who confess one God who is Father, Son, and Holy Spirit, whose being and works are inseparable and must be understood in light of each other. But in fact churches in the Reformed tradition (not to mention churches in some other Christian traditions) have traditionally neglected their own doctrine of the Trinity when they have talked about the Holy Spirit. Apart from a few words about how the Spirit inspired the writing of scripture and illuminates the minds of its readers to understand it, and apart from a few brief references to the Spirit's speaking through the prophets and presence in Jesus, Reformed churches and their confessions have often implied that there *was* no Holy Spirit until the third member of the Trinity joined the team at Pentecost. Indeed, many Christians believe that the Spirit begins to work for the first time when they have an immediate personal experience of the Spirit's presence and work in their individual lives.

How would we understand the person and work of the Spirit, and therefore the meaning of true spirituality, if we remembered that the Spirit is the Spirit of the God who is the world's Creator and Preserver, who was at work in the history of Israel, who came not only sometime *after* but was present and at work *in* Jesus? What, in short, if we had a *Trinitarian* understanding of the Holy Spirit and Christian spirituality?

Our first consideration must be the Trinitarian identity of the Spirit herself/itself/himself. (The word *spirit* is feminine in Old Testament Hebrew, neuter in New Testament Greek, and masculine in the Latin of the ancient church.) This will lead us to look at consequences of faith in the Spirit for the meaning of "spiritual renewal" in the lives of individual Christians, in the church, and in a world hungry for genuine spirituality.[1]

Who Is the Holy Spirit?

A Trinitarian approach to the question requires us to pay more attention than has the traditional doctrine of the Holy Spirit to the work of the Spirit of God in the Old Testament. It also enables us to discover in the New Testament some aspects of the Spirit's identity and work that traditional doctrine has neglected or obscured.

The Spirit
of the God of Israel

The Old Testament tells us several things about the Spirit of God that Christians who think exclusively of the Holy Spirit in the New Testament are prone to forget.

The Spirit's Work in Creation

The Spirit is at work in God's creation and preservation of the world and all life in it—first of all simply physical, creaturely life. Wherever there is life instead of death in human beings and in their natural environment, and wherever creaturely life is respected, preserved, and defended, there Christians recognize the creative, life-giving Spirit of God at work (Gen. 1:2; 2:7; Pss. 33:6; 104:30; Job 33:4).

The Spirit's Work
in Human Creativity

The Spirit of God is the source of all human culture, art, creative skill, intelligence, and wisdom. So, for instance, in Exodus 31:3–5, the Lord says of one Bezalel, "I have filled him with divine spirit, with ability, intelligence, and knowledge in every kind of craft, to devise artistic designs, to work in gold, silver, and bronze, in cutting stones for setting, and in carving wood, in every kind of craft."[2] Calvin picked up this emphasis when he spoke of "those most excellent benefits of the divine Spirit" that God "distributes to whomever he will" (including the "ungodly" who work in secular arts and sciences) "for the common good of mankind." "If we regard the Spirit of God as the sole fountain of truth, we shall neither reject the truth itself, nor despise it *wherever* it shall appear, unless we wish to dishonor the Spirit of God."[3]

The Spirit's Work in the Achievement of Justice

The Spirit is the Spirit of the God who is especially on the side of all who are helpless, wretched, and oppressed because they have been forgotten or excluded by the rich and powerful (Pss. 103:6; 146). The Spirit of the Lord is therefore "in" or "upon" leaders and prophets who demand political, economic, and social justice for the victims of injustice (Isa. 11:1ff.; 61:1ff.). Wherever such justice is done in the world (even if it is done by those who do not "know" God), there God's Spirit is at work. And wherever such justice is *not* done (even if those who allow or cause it are pious believers), there the Spirit of the Lord is absent or at least resisted.

Jesus said that the Spirit "blows where it wills" (John 3:8), and the Old Testament tells us that may mean outside what we call the "religious" sphere, wherever, by whomever, the physical health and wholeness of human beings and their natural environment are valued and protected; wherever, in whomever, wisdom, beauty, creativity, and truth are manifest; and wherever, by whomever, justice is done for the wretched of the earth. This is true whether or not there is a "personal religious experience" of the Spirit's presence and work. For the Holy Spirit is the Spirit of the God who is Creator, Preserver, and Defender of the life and welfare of *all* God's creation and *all* God's creatures.

The Holy Spirit and Jesus

According to the New Testament, if we want to know who the Holy Spirit is and what the Spirit does, we have to look first of all not at this or that Spirit-filled Christian but at Jesus of Nazareth. At every point in Jesus' life, in everything he said and did, he was filled, led, inspired, and empowered by God's Spirit.

Jesus was conceived by the Spirit (Matt. 1:20). At his baptism the Spirit descended upon him (Matt. 3:16). By the power of the Spirit he healed the sick, spoke with authority, cast out demonic forces that destroyed people's minds and bodies (Matt. 12:28), and brought good news of liberation to the poor and oppressed (Luke 4:18). If we want to know what it means to have the Spirit dwell within us, the Gospels say, look at Jesus. He is our prime example of the life of a Spirit-filled person.

And what kind of life is that? Not the kind of life people in his time (or in ours) expected of a "spiritual" person. He went to parties, ate and drank, and had a good time. He talked more about how people got their money and what they did with it than about their sexual purity. He was as interested in the health of their bodies as in the state of their souls.

He was the friend and associate not just of pious and morally respectable people but also of immoral, unbelieving sinners. He defended the cause of those who were rejected by polite society and despised by the religious establishment. He believed that human need takes precedence over strict conformity to the law. He came to *serve* other people, not to assert his moral and religious superiority over them.

He loved his own and God's enemies and did good to those who hated him. He trusted and served the God he called Father even when it did not pay off in personal success and happiness. He prayed even when everything he had worked and hoped for was denied him and he felt forsaken by God. He did not come just to make people "feel good" and give them everything they wanted; he came to tell them about the coming rule of God's justice and compassion in the world, and to invite them to *give up* everything they had to follow him in costly service of this coming kingdom.

His is the kind of life that is the result of God's Holy Spirit coming to dwell in a person. If we want to know who the Holy Spirit is and what the Spirit does, and therefore what a truly Spirit-filled person or a Spirit-filled community looks like, we have to look first of all at *him*. The Spirit is by definition the Spirit who dwelt *in* Jesus, comes *from* him, and continues the work he began.

The Unique Work of the Spirit

The Holy Spirit is the Spirit of God the Creator and Lord of Israel, and the Spirit at work in the life, death, resurrection, and living presence of Jesus Christ. But I agree with Berkhof's argument that, contrary to the teaching of most theologians in the Reformed tradition from Calvin to Barth, the Spirit is not just the agent or instrument of the Father and the Son but does something that is the Spirit's own unique work.[4] I think that it can be summarized with the word *new*.

The Holy Spirit brings new creaturely life that is stronger than sickness and even death itself. The Spirit makes possible new beginnings in the lives of people whose lives seem to be at a dead end. The Spirit brings new truth and guidance from God. According to Paul, the Spirit not only enables us to put aside the sins of so-called bad people, such as fornication, licentiousness, drunkenness, and carousing (though in our time it is still necessary to emphasize these sins too!); the Spirit also enables us to put aside the sins of seemingly good people, such as enmity, strife, jealousy, anger, quarrels, dissension, factions, envy, bitterness, wrangling, slander, and malice (sins not unknown in some churches today). The Holy Spirit creates (even in the church!) new people whose lives are marked by joy, peace, patience, kindness, generosity, faithfulness, gentleness, and self-control (Gal. 5:16ff., Eph. 4:31ff.). The Holy Spirit calls together, holds together, and sends out a new reconciled community that is an agent of reconciliation in the world outside the church.

When the Holy Spirit breaks in, old ways of thinking and living are left behind and new ways of thinking and living begin to take over. Old boring, oppressive, and dead social structures and religious institutions are transformed into new exciting, liberating ones. It may not happen all at once, but when the Holy Spirit comes, a new day dawns, and with it hope for a different future not only for individual Christians and the Christian community but for the world, with courage and strength to move toward it.

People who like things the way they are (or used to be), who benefit from the status quo in church and world, who therefore value stability, permanence, decency and order above everything else—such people are suspicious and afraid of the Holy Spirit, and too much talk about the Spirit makes them nervous and defensive. But people who suffer and see no way out of suffering, who are enslaved and oppressed by their own and others' sinfulness and injustice—they yearn for the coming of the Spirit. For the Spirit is not just the Lord and Giver of life but the Lord and Giver of *new* life—to individuals, to churches, and to political, social, and economic structures.

Christian Spirituality

Now what does Christian spirituality look like when it is based
on such a Trinitarian doctrine of the Holy Spirit? Although much
more needs to be said, it has five characteristics that in my opinion especially need to be emphasized in order to correct some common mis-
understandings of spirituality among Christians in our time, and to offer an alternative to self-defeating ways in which spiritually hungry
people inside as well as outside the church seek to satisfy their
hunger.[5]

God-Centered Life

A long tradition that began in classical Roman Catholicism and
has continued to be popular among Protestants, as well as among
seekers for a new spirituality outside the church, assumes that spiritual renewal begins by looking deep within our own souls and our private religious experience. It begins with self-examination. Behind
this assumption is the belief of the ancient Greeks that the human soul
is a little bit of God in us, so that to get in touch with *ourselves* at the
deepest level is to get in touch with *God* or the Spirit of God.

It is, of course, true that God's Spirit comes to dwell within us.
But as we have seen, it is not necessarily the presence of the Holy
Spirit we discover when we analyze and meditate on our own inner
selves and personal religious experience; it may be only our own finite and often sinful human feelings, longings, and ambitions. If we
want to distinguish between God's Spirit and our own spirits, we have
to look at what *scripture* tells us about who the Spirit is and what the
Spirit says and does. That means (in direct contrast to many programs
of spiritual development within as well as outside the church today)
that if we want to recognize and experience the presence of God's
life-renewing Spirit *in* us, we must first look *away* from ourselves, *beyond* our personal experience.

If we want to know what the Spirit of God is doing and promises
to do in our lives, we cannot simply analyze and tell our own little stories or listen to those of others; we must interpret our stories in light
of *God's* story with ancient Israel and the first Christian community.[6]
If we want to know what it would mean for us to be truly spiritual persons, we must first of all look at the life of Jesus and the kind of person *he* was, not at our own lives and the kind of persons we would

like to be. If it is genuine Christian spirituality and not some kind of self-concocted spirituality we want, we must first of all follow Calvin's advice to "get out of ourselves," "forget ourselves."[7] We must stop circling round and round our own personal feelings, needs, problems, fears, and hopes—even our own or someone else's "spiritual journey." We must first of all let ourselves be told something we cannot tell ourselves about the work of the Spirit of the triune God of the Bible who does indeed come *to* us but not *from* us, who does not belong to us but to whom we belong.

The first thing to be said about Christian spirituality, then, is that it is not self-centered (not even *Christian* self-centered) but God- and Christ-centered. We need not be afraid that we and our personal experience will be left out if we forget ourselves at least for a few minutes now and then to focus on what the Bible and a biblically based doctrine of the Trinity tell us about who the Spirit is and what the Spirit does. For the Holy Spirit is the Spirit of a God who cares for each of us, knows better than we what we need most, and promises to be present and at work in our lives just as we *give up* self-centered preoccupation with ourselves and our little life stories to remember who it is from whom our help comes.

Life in and for the World

Some Christians, as well as others, think that to be "born again of the Spirit" means to experience renewal that is purely private and religious. For them spiritual life has to do only with prayer, meditation, and seeking guidance from reading the Bible and other inspirational books. It has to do with feeling the presence of God when we withdraw from the everyday world and from association with unbelieving, sinful people, to commune with God alone or in the company of a few other people seeking spiritual renewal. It has nothing to do with such "unspiritual" things as bodily needs and pleasures, how we make and spend money, or our social–political commitments. It seeks to rise above all that into the higher and purer life of the soul.

There are indeed times (regular times) when, like Jesus, we need to withdraw to spend time alone with God, seeking the comforting and renewing presence of God's Spirit in our lives. But the triune God into whose presence we come and whose Spirit we seek is a *this-worldly* God. This is the God who created, blesses, protects, and defends the creaturely life of all God's creatures. This God is at work to establish just social conditions that provide for the welfare especially of those who are most unable to care for themselves and their families. This God came to us in a flesh-and-blood human being who was not the enemy but the friend of worldly sinners, who gave his life to reconcile all kinds of people to one another as well as to God. This God promises not only a new heaven but a new *earth*.

Truly spiritual people, therefore, are not recognized by how suspicious they are of physical needs and pleasures (especially sex), but by how joyfully, thankfully, and responsibly they acknowledge them as good gifts of God. They are recognized not only by how much they pray, but also by how much they pray for a sinful and suffering world. They are recognized not only by how much they "praise the Lord" for "what the Lord has done for me," but also by how sensitive their praise makes them to the needs and hurts of other people. They are recognized not only by how much time they spend reading the Bible and other devotional literature, but also by the way their reading influences their business practices, political decisions, family and social relationships. They are recognized not only by their testimonies to how God befriended them and came to their aid when they were lost sinners who did not deserve it, but also by the way they befriend and come to the aid of other lost sinners who do not deserve it.

Any spirituality, including supposedly Christian spirituality, that retreats from the world into the self-serving piety of a private religious life is a false spirituality that flees rather than seeks God. True Christian spirituality cheerfully and confidently plunges into the life of our dirty, sinful, confused world, for there is where we meet the Spirit of the triune God who is present and at work not to save people *from* but *in* and *for the sake of* that world—the world that was and is and will be God's world.

Ordinary Daily Life

Some people expect and find evidence of the Spirit's work only when they experience (often through the agency of other people of great faith and charismatic power) the supernatural intervention of a God who comes to our aid when all human wisdom, resources, and possibilities have been exhausted. Of course God's powerful Spirit can and does work in such inexplicable, miraculous ways.

Christians who know the Spirit of the triune God of the Bible, however, also expect and find the work of the Spirit in ordinary, everyday human experience, when there seems to be no supernatural intervention. They recognize and thank God for the life-giving power of God's Spirit when health is restored and life is saved in a hospital by the scientific knowledge and skill of doctors and nurses who may or may not be Christians or even "religious" people at all. They recognize and thank God for the justice-bringing work of God's Spirit when they see justice done by a secular court of law or a governmental body (sometimes despite the *indifference* or *opposition* of some very "spiritual" Christians and churches). They recognize and thank God for the work of the Spirit of the risen Christ when alienated marriage partners are reconciled—even when it happens through the mediation of an agnostic or atheist therapist. They rejoice and their faith is strengthened wherever, through whomever, they see evidence of God's creative, liberating, reconciling, life-renewing Spirit at work. And they gladly join hands to cooperate also with non-Christians or questionable Christians through whom they see their God at work, grateful that everything does not depend on us Christians and our church.

It is a sign of *false* spirituality and a *weak* faith when Christians are unwilling and unable to recognize the work of the Holy Spirit in ordinary processes of everyday life as well as in miraculous interruptions of it, through people who do not even know by whose Spirit it is that they know what they know and do what they do as well as through Christians of great faith and charismatic power. For as the Declaration of Faith puts it, "The Holy Spirit is free" and "works beyond the church even among those we suspect or scorn" (5.7).[8]

Life That Endures
with Hope for the Future

The spirituality of some Christians, and some others as well, is based on experiences of how God has helped them to solve insoluble problems, saved them or their loved ones from sickness and trouble, given them what they prayed for, made everything come out right. Their faith is strong so long as they can bear witness to such experiences, but without them their faith crumbles.

Spirituality that depends on success stories is shallow and inevitably short-lived. Genuine Christian spirituality is that of people who are indeed grateful for concrete, visible signs of the life-giving work of the Spirit in their lives and in the lives of others, but whose faith does not depend on these signs. It is spirituality like that of Jesus, who prayed and entrusted his life to God even as he suffered and died feeling totally Godforsaken. It is spirituality like that of the apostle Paul and countless Christians through the centuries, who have understood that like their crucified Lord they and their loved ones were not to be spared the hardship, suffering, and dying that is the lot of all finite creatures. It is the spirituality of Christians who understand that for them as for Christ himself *added* hardship and suffering comes to those who serve the unqualified compassion and unrelenting demand for the justice of the kingdom of God that breaks into a hostile world. (It is my impression that Christians in this country and around the world who have the least and suffer most often understand this better than many of us more fortunate and affluent Christians who are prone to whine and complain when God does not give us everything we want.)

True spirituality is the spirituality of Christians who know that in the "sufferings of this present time" the Spirit does not always save us and others *from* our weakness but "helps us *in* our weakness," to give us the comfort, courage, and strength to endure as we entrust our own lives to God and share the suffering of others, knowing that whatever happens, good or bad, nothing can separate us or anyone else from the love of God in Jesus Christ our Lord (Rom. 8:18–39).

True spirituality is not based and does not depend on present experience of the power of God's Spirit over sickness, suffering, and death. It is based on and lives by memory of what the God who raised Jesus from the dead has done in the past, and is therefore sure hope for what the life-giving power of the Spirit of God who is stronger than death itself will do in the future—for us, for our loved ones, and for all people everywhere.

Life Together

Authentic Christian spirituality is born, nourished, and fulfilled in the Christian community for the sake of its witness in word and action to the presence and work of the living triune God in the world. We look back now to where we started, by considering the unique place and responsibility of the church in a pluralistic society.[9]

Like many people outside the church today, many Christians are suspicious of "organized religion" and "the institutional church." They experience the church's worship as lifeless, boring, and irrelevant to their daily lives. They hear in its preaching, teaching, and official "position papers" a defense of this or that liberal or conservative political ideology rather than the proclamation of the gospel of Jesus Christ. They believe its leadership is more likely to echo the moral confusion of our time than to offer true spiritual guidance to people trying to find their way in it. They suspect that its membership is made up of merely "nominal" Christians whose lives have not been transformed by the renewing power of the Holy Spirit. They see the Christian community torn apart by the same power struggles between competing groups that are destroying contemporary secular society.

Such people often think that they have one of two alternatives if they want to discover and live by the presence of God in their lives: They must withdraw from a compromised and corrupt church into a purely private religious life. Or they must form or join a small group of "real Christians" outside or within the church whose religious experience is like their own, who share their particular understanding of authentic biblical-Christian faith and life, and who agree with their liberal, conservative, or evangelical position on social and political issues.

I believe that we must take such criticisms of the church very seriously. But people who are too spiritual for the church are also too spiritual for the triune God who promises to be present and at work in this all-too-questionable Christian community.

Jesus promised to send the Spirit of God who dwelt in him not to isolated individuals but to the *community* of his followers—beginning with the very ones he *condemned* for arguing about who would be greatest in the coming kingdom, who had denied and deserted him when they discovered that following him did not lead to personal power, prestige, and success but to costly discipleship. That promise was fulfilled at Pentecost when "they were all together in one place" (Acts 2:1).

The apostle Paul knew something about churches in which there are all kinds of personal immorality, vicious power struggles for control, wrangling about what kinds of people are to be included or excluded, and bickering about who is and who is not a real Christian. But Paul said that the gifts of the Spirit, which are indeed given to individual Christians, are given them not just for their personal benefit and enjoyment but for the "common good" of just such a community (1 Cor. 12:7). He said that different gifts are given to different kinds of people (Jews and Gentiles, slave and free, men and women), and that they themselves as well as the church as a whole need this variety (Rom. 12:5ff.; 1 Cor. 12:12ff.). He said that these gifts include not only such supernatural gifts as healing, miracle-working, and speaking in tongues; but also such ordinary gifts as preaching, teaching, helping people in need, and church leadership (RSV: "administration"!), which are functions precisely of what we call the "institutional" church (1 Cor. 12:27–31).

The writer of Ephesians emphasizes that the gifts of the Spirit are given not just to "build up" individual Christians but to build up the whole body of Christ—and that not just for the community's own benefit but to "equip the saints" (all of them *sinful* saints) for the work of their common ministry in and for the world (Eph. 1:3ff.; 4:12ff.).[10]

When spiritually hungry Christians withdraw from the church with all its weaknesses and faults to attend to their own spiritual development alone or in the company of others whose religious experience, understanding of Christian faith and life, and ideological commitments are just like their own, they deprive themselves *and* others of the very Spirit of God they yearn for. According to the New Testament, the Holy Spirit is the liberating, reconciling, transforming Spirit of the risen Christ who is promised to the *community* of Christians—a community of ordinary, sinful people who are *different* from one another, who in the surrounding world may be *enemies* of one another. They are promised the gifts of the Spirit first of all to enable *them* to live together in mutual openness, to learn from one another and care for one another. And they are promised the gifts of the Spirit to enable them to be ambassadors of God-in-Christ to overcome the "us–them" mentality that in the world outside the church creates hostile rivalries between people who differ from one another in gender, race, class, religious experience, understanding of the moral life, and political agendas.[11]

How can Christians expect to experience the reconciling presence and work of *this* Spirit in their own lives if they are unable and unwilling to live in community even with fellow Christians who are different from themselves (not to mention other people)? How can they expect people outside the church to be impressed by their witness to the reconciling power of God's Spirit if they themselves only echo the us-versus-them mentality that divides the world into angry competing camps?

How can Christians hope to receive the Spirit's gift of love (by definition the mutual love of people who are different from one another) if they cannot or will not love even fellow Christians who are different from themselves? How can they expect outsiders to be impressed by their talk about Christian love if they are unwilling and unable to demonstrate it even in their own community?

How can Christians expect the Spirit's guidance in the theological and ethical decisions they have to make if they are willing to listen only to people who agree with what they already think, if they are unwilling and unable to learn from fellow Christians who have come to a different understanding of Christian faith and life after they too have sought the Spirit's guidance, read the same Bible, and sought to follow the same Christ? How can they expect others to be open to learn new truth that comes from God if they themselves are not willing to learn it?

To withdraw from the church into a purely private "me and God" relationship or to associate only with a few "real Christians" just like me is to reject the very gifts of the Spirit we seek for ourselves, and to belie the very promise of the transforming power of the Spirit we proclaim to the world.

In our time there is indeed a desperate hunger for a new spirituality that breathes new life into the deadness of our individual lives, the church, and the world around us. But that hunger cannot be satisfied by seeking escape from the Christian community into the kind of narcissistic, self-righteous false spirituality that is popular in the church as well as in our secular society today.

True spirituality comes only as Christians are not too "spiritual" to open themselves to recognize the promised presence and work of the Holy Spirit in and through the not-always-very-exciting and in fact sometimes pretty boring and routine preaching, teaching, worship, and sacramental observances of the church. Authentic spiritual renewal comes only in the church's constant struggle to *become* a community of liberal, conservative, and evangelical men and women, with different racial, class, and cultural identities, who are liberated, reconciled, and transformed to establish a true "communion of the Holy Spirit"—one that exists not just for their own benefit, but in order to participate in the liberating, reconciling, transforming work of the triune God they confess in and for the world.

Christians and the Christian church can do nothing more faithful *and* more relevant than to give themselves to *that* kind of spiritual renewal and *that* kind of spiritual development.

Notes

Notes for Introduction

1. Jürgen Moltmann, *The Crucified God* (New York: Harper & Row, 1974), 7.
2. David Tracy, *The Analogical Imagination* (New York: Crossroad, 1981), 4ff.
3. *The Book of Confessions of the Presbyterian Church (U.S.A.)* and *A Declaration of Faith* are published by the Office of the General Assembly, 100 Witherspoon Street, Louisville, Kentucky 40202-1396. *The Book of Confessions* will sometimes be cited as *BC*. A collection of some of the most important classical Reformed confessional statements may be found in Philip Schaff, *Creeds of Christendom,* vol. III (Grand Rapids: Baker Book House, 1966). Lukas Vischer has collected twentieth-century confessional statements of Reformed churches around the world (including *A Declaration of Faith*) in *Reformed Witness Today: A Collection of Confessions and Statements of Faith Issued by Reformed Churches* (Bern: Evangelische Arbeitsstelle Oekumene Schweiz, 1982). Confessions cited in this book may be found in one or more of these sources.
4. The third and fourth ordination vows for elders, deacons, and ministers in the Presbyterian Church (U.S.A.) read as follows: "Do you sincerely receive and adopt the essential tenets of the Reformed faith as expressed in the confessions of our Church as authentic and reliable expositions of what Scripture leads us to believe and do, and will you be instructed and led by those confessions as you lead the people of God?" "Will you fulfill your office [be a minister of the Word and Sacrament] in obedience to Jesus Christ, under the authority of Scripture, and [be] continually guided by our confessions?" (Book of Order, G-14.0207, G-14.0405).

Notes for Chapter 1

1. See Karl Barth's criticism of "pious egocentricity" in *Church Dogmatics* IV/3, 566ff. (Barth's *Church Dogmatics* is a multivolume work published by T & T Clark, Edinburgh, 1936–1966.)
2. See, for instance, James Cone: "And maybe our white theologians are right when they insist that I have overlooked the *universal* significance of Jesus' message. But I contend that there is no universalism that is not particular. Indeed their insistence upon the universal note of the gospel arises out of their own particular political and social interests. As long as they can be sure that the gospel is *for everybody,* ignoring that God liberated a *particular* people from Egypt, came in a particular man called Jesus, and for the particular purpose of liberating the oppressed, then they can continue to talk in theological abstractions, failing to recognize that such talk is not the gospel unless it is related to the concrete freedom of the little ones" (in *God of the Oppressed* [New York: Harper & Row, 1978], 137).
3. The works of William C. Placher, *Unapologetic Theology: A Christian Voice in a Pluralistic Conversation* (Louisville, Ky.: Westminster John Knox Press, 1989) and Lesslie Newbigin, *The gospel in a Pluralistic Society* (Grand Rapids: Wm. B. Eerdmans Publishing Co., 1989) have been a source of invaluable help as I set out to fulfill this task.

Notes for Chapter 2

1. Karl Barth, *Dogmatics in Outline* (New York: Philosophical Library, 1949), 9.
2. Benjamin A. Reist, *Processive Revelation* (Louisville, Ky.: Westminster John Knox Press, 1992), 32f.
3. Reist, *Processive Revelation,* 34.
4. For a more developed discussion of the distinctive place of the Reformed confessional tradition among other Christian traditions, see *The Confessional Nature of the Church,* a study paper approved by the 198th General Assembly of the Presbyterian Church (U.S.A.) in 1986 *Minutes of the General Assembly,* Part I, 515ff.
5. Karl Barth, "The Desirability and Possibility of a Universal Reformed Creed," an address given in 1925, published in *Theology and the Church* (New York: Harper & Row, 1962), 117.
6. During the eighteenth and nineteenth centuries, Reformed Christians influenced by Protestant orthodoxy believed that no new confessions were needed and could in fact only water down or compromise earlier confessional statements, which they were sure had already reformed the church once and for all time. More liberal Reformed Christians

influenced by the Enlightenment were opposed to new confessions because their commitment to freedom of thought made them suspicious
of all confessional restraint.

7. Lukas Vischer, ed., *Reformed Witness Today: A Collection of Confessions and Statements of Faith Issued by Reformed Churches.*

8. Barth, *Theology and the Church,* 112, 114.

9. Barth, *Theology and the Church,* 117.

10. The original version of the Scots Confession may be found in Philip
Schaff, *The Creeds of Christendom,* vol. III, 436. Other statements in
Reformed confessions that subject the church's confessions to criticism and correction in light of the higher authority of scripture: Westminster Confession, I.10; Preface to the Confession of 1967; Declaration of Faith, 6.3; Statement of Faith (1958) of the Church of Jesus
Christ in Madagascar, Art. 4.

11. The rule that scripture is to be interpreted by scripture is found
in Scots Confession, Chap. XVIII; Second Helvetic Confession,
Chap. II; Westminster Confession, I.7, 9; Declaration of Faith, 6.3;
Basic Confession (1979) of the Karo-Batak Protestant Church, Art.
1.d.

12. On Calvin's recognition of the Christological interpretation of scripture: "In our reading of Scripture we shall hold simply to that which
speaks clearly and definitely to our conscience and makes us feel that
it leads us to Christ" (*Commentary on John* 12:48). "The letter, therefore, is dead, and the law of the Lord slays its readers, where it both is
cut off from Christ's grace (2 Cor. 3:6) and, leaving the heart untouched, sounds in the ears alone. But if through the Spirit it is really
branded upon hearts, if it shows forth Christ, it is the word of life" (*Institutes,* I.9.3).

13. For a brief description of Calvin's literary-historical interpretation of
scripture, see William J. Bouwsma, *John Calvin: A Sixteenth-Century
Portrait* (New York: Oxford University Press, 1988), 113ff. The Second Helvetic Confession says that an "orthodox and genuine" interpretation of the scriptures must pay attention to "the nature of the language in which they were written" and "the circumstances in which
they were set down" (Chap. II).

14. So also the New Confession (1972) of the Presbyterian Church in the
Republic of Korea: "The Scriptures are dependent upon the time,
place and condition in which the writers lived, so scripture can be understood and interpreted rightly only through accurate study of the
grammar, the thought patterns of the respective languages and the
conditions—societal, historical, cultural—in which the writers lived"
(I.4).

Notes for Chapter 3

1. Jürgen Moltmann, *The Trinity and the Kingdom* (San Francisco: Harper & Row, 1981); Daniel L. Migliore, *Faith Seeking Understanding* (Grand Rapids: Wm. B. Eerdmans Publishing Co., 1991); William C. Placher, *Narratives of a Vulnerable God* (Louisville, Ky.: Westminster John Knox Press, 1994); Karl Rahner, *The Trinity* (New York: Herder & Herder, 1970); Leonardo Boff, *Trinity and Society* (Maryknoll, N.Y.: Orbis Books, 1988); Catherine Mowry LaCugna, *God for Us: The Trinity and Christian Life* (San Francisco: Harper San Francisco, 1991); Eberhard Jüngel, *The Doctrine of the Trinity: God's Being Is in Becoming* (Grand Rapids: Wm. B. Eerdmans Publishing Co., 1976); Wolfhart Pannenberg, *Systematic Theology*, vol. I (Grand Rapids: Wm. B. Eerdmans Publishing Co., 1991); Ted Peters, *God as Trinity* (Louisville, Ky.: Westminster John Knox Press, 1993); Robert Jenson, *The Triune Identity: God According to the Gospel* (Philadelphia: Fortress Press, 1982).

2. See Scots Confession, Chap. I; Second Helvetic Confession, Chap. III; Westminster Confession, Chap. II. For a summary description of the doctrine of the Trinity in the confessions of classical Reformed tradition see Jan Rohls, *Theologie reformierter Bekenntnisschriften* (Göttingen: Vandenhoeck & Ruprecht, 1987), 53ff.

3. The Heidelberg Catechism begins with a confession of Jesus Christ as our only comfort in life and in death (Q.1), and defines God the Father Almighty as "the eternal Father of our Lord Jesus Christ" (Q.26). In a similar way the Geneva Catechism says that we know who God is and how rightly to honor, serve, and trust God "by his Word, in which he declares his mercy to us in Christ, and assures us of his love toward us" (Q.13).

4. For some typical examples of this now common and familiar criticism of the traditional doctrine of the Trinity, see Jürgen Moltmann, *The Trinity and the Kingdom*, 191ff.; Leonardo Boff, *Trinity and Society*, 16ff.; Sallie McFague, *Models of God: Theology for an Ecological, Nuclear Age* (Philadelphia: Fortress Press, 1987), 63ff.; John Douglas Hall, *Professing the Faith: Christian Theology in a North American Context* (Minneapolis: Fortress Press, 1993), chaps. 2, 3.

5. On the split between the sovereign power and love of God, see Jürgen Moltmann, *The Crucified God* (New York: Harper & Row, 1973), chap. 5.

6. On the split between God's work in the world and God's work in the church, see Clark H. Pinnock, *A Wideness in God's Mercy* (Grand Rapids: Zondervan Publishing House, 1992), especially chaps. 3–5.

7. So, for instance: Confession of 1967, United Presbyterian Church in the U.S.A.; Declaration of Faith, Presbyterian Church in the United

States (1976); Statement of Faith, Church of Jesus Christ in Madagascar (1958); Theological Declaration, Broederkring of the Dutch Reformed Church of South Africa (1979); Declaration of Faith for the
Church in South Africa, Presbyterian Church of South Africa (1973);
A Common Comprehension of Faith, Council of Churches in Indone-
sia (1967); Confession of the Church of Toraja (1981); New Confession, Presbyterian Church in the Republic of Korea (1972); Confession
of Faith, Presbyterian-Reformed Church in Cuba (1977); A Declaration of Faith, Congregational Church in England and Wales (1967).

8. On the presence and work of the triune God in the world and the
church's mission in the world see, for instance, Confession of 1967
(*BC*, 9.07, 9.10, 9.17, 9.25, 9.31, 9.41–47). See also the Declaration of
Faith (1.5, 2.3, 5.5, 7.3–4, 8.1–5, 10.2, 5), and Declaration of Faith of
the Congregational Church in England and Wales (1967), III.6.

9. Moltmann, *The Trinity and the Kingdom*, 174ff.; Boff, *Trinity and So-
ciety*, 93ff., 134ff.; LaCugna, *God for Us: The Trinity and Christian
Life*, 270ff. See also LaCugna's article "God in Communion with Us,"
included in a collection of essays edited by her, *Freeing Theology: The
Essentials of Theology in Feminist Perspective* (San Francisco: Harper
San Francisco, 1993), 83ff.

10. A perichoretic understanding of the Trinity relativizes the traditional
gender-specific understanding of the relation between the Father and
Son even when it still uses it. Moltmann quotes the Council of Toledo
in 1675, which said, "It must be held that the Son was created, neither
out of nothingness nor yet out of any substance, but that He was begotten or born out of the Father's womb (*de utero Patris*), that is, out
of his very essence" (*The Trinity and the Kingdom*, 165). This leads
Moltmann to say that we have to understand the Father as a "motherly
Father" (p. 164). Boff speaks of a "maternal Father and a paternal
Mother" (*Trinity and Society*, 120f.).

11. An exception is the Declaration of Faith, 5.8: "We affirm the unity of
God's being and work. We may not separate the work of God as Creator from the work of God as Redeemer. We may not set the Son's love
against the Father's justice. We may not value the Holy Spirit's work
above the work of the Father and Son. The Father, the Son and the Holy
Spirit are one God."

Notes for Chapter 4

1. Sallie McFague, *Models of God: Theology for an Ecological, Nuclear
Age* (Philadelphia: Fortress Press, 1987), 63ff.; Leonardo Boff, *Trin-
ity and Society* (Maryknoll, N.Y.: Orbis Books, 1988), 13ff.; Douglas
John Hall, *Professing the Faith* (Minneapolis: Fortress Press, 1993),

92–130; Jürgen Moltmann, *The Trinity and the Kingdom* (San Francisco: Harper & Row, 1981), 192ff.

2. In *John Calvin: A Sixteenth Century Portrait* (New York: Oxford University Press, 1988), William J. Bouwsma argues that there are "two Calvins, coexisting uncomfortably within the same historical personage" (p. 230). The first is the humanistic, evangelical, biblical Calvin, the second the rationalistic, scholastic Calvin. See especially chaps. 6, 7, and 15. In a similar way Alexandre Ganoczy, *The Young Calvin* (Philadelphia: Westminster Press, 1987), argues that there is both an open, prophetic, pastoral, ecumenical, Christ-centered Calvin; and an intolerant, austere, militant anti-catholic Calvin. See pp. 307ff. Following Ganoczy, John de Gruchy, *Liberating Reformed Theology: A South African Contribution to Ecumenical Debate* (Grand Rapids: Wm. B. Eerdmans Publishing Co., 1991), distinguishes between the "young " Calvin, who is the origin of an evangelical, liberating, transforming Calvinism; and the "older" Calvin, who is the origin of a dominating, constrictive "imperial Calvinism." See pp. 17–21, 114–18.

3. de Gruchy, *Liberating Reformed Theology,* 127.

4. All quotations from Calvin's *Institutes of the Christian Religion* are from The Library of Christian Classics, vol. XXI, edited by John T. McNeill and translated by Ford L. Battles (Philadelphia: Westminster Press, 1960).

5. Although the Heidelberg Catechism is more aware than other early Reformed confessions that God the Creator is the "Father of our Lord Jesus Christ" (Q.26) and "our faithful God and Father" (Q.28), it too says that the "providence of God" means "the almighty and ever-present power of God whereby he still upholds, as it were by his own hand, heaven and earth together with all creatures, and rules in such a way that leaves and grass, rain and drought, fruitful and unfruitful years, food and drink, health and sickness, riches and poverty, and everything else come to us not by chance but by his fatherly hand" (Q.27).

6. See Second Helvetic Confession, Chap. XI: "We do not in any way teach that the divine nature in Christ has suffered."

7. See Moltmann, *The Trinity and the Kingdom,* 194ff.

8. See Karl Barth, *The Humanity of God* (Richmond: John Knox Press, 1960), 37ff.; Moltmann, *The Trinity and the Kingdom,* 194ff.; Daniel L. Migliore, *The Power of God* (Philadelphia: Westminster Press, 1983).

9. In his commentary on Colossians 1:15, Calvin wrote: "The sum is, that God in Himself, that is, in his naked majesty, is invisible; not only to the physical eyes but also to human understanding; and that He is revealed to us in Christ alone, where we may behold Him as in a mirror.

For in Christ He shows us his righteousness, goodness, wisdom, power, in short, His entire self. We must, therefore, take care not to seek Him elsewhere; for outside Christ, everything that claims to represent God will be an idol" (quoted in de Gruchy, *Liberating Reformed Theology*, 118–19).

10. See Barth, *Church Dogmatics* II/1, par. 28, "The Being of God as the One Who Loves in Freedom," 257–321.
11. Barth, *The Humanity of God*; Moltmann, *The Crucified God* (New York: Harper & Row, 1973); Hall, *Professing the Faith*.
12. The Declaration of Faith (4.6) puts it this way: "We recognize the work of God in Jesus' power and authority. He did what only God can do. We also recognize the work of God in Jesus' lowliness. When he lived as a servant and went humbly to his death, the greatness that belongs only to God was manifest. In both his majesty and lowliness, Jesus is the eternal Son of God, God himself with us."
13. See Moltmann, *The Crucified God,* 222.
14. See Barth, *Church Dogmatics* IV/3, second half, 644.
15. Declaration of Faith, 10.4: "We know our efforts cannot bring in God's kingdom. But hope plunges us into the struggle for victories over evil that are possible now in the world, the church, and our individual lives. Hope gives us courage and energy to contend against all opposition, however invincible it may seem, for the new world and the new humanity that are surely coming. Jesus is Lord! He has been Lord from the beginning. He will be Lord at the end. Even now he is Lord."

Notes for Chapter 5

1. See Lesslie Newbigin, *The gospel in a Pluralistic Society* (Grand Rapids: Wm. B. Eerdmans Publishing Co., 1989), chap. 14; Schubert M. Ogden, *Is There Only One True Religion or Are There Many?* (Dallas, Tex.: Southern Methodist University Press, 1992); Clark H. Pinnock, *A Wideness in God's Mercy* (Grand Rapids: Zondervan Publishing House, 1992); Carl E. Braaten, *No Other gospel!* (Minneapolis: Fortress Press, 1992); Paul F. Knitter, *No Other Name?* (Maryknoll, N.Y.: Orbis Books, 1990).
2. See Knitter, *No Other Name?* 231.
3. See Karl Rahner, "Christianity and the Non-Christian Religions," in *Theological Investigations,* vol. 5 (Baltimore: Helicon, 1966). See also the discussions of Rahner's position in Newbigin, *gospel in a Pluralistic Society,* 174ff.; Knitter, *No Other Name?* 125ff.
4. Barth, *Church Dogmatics* IV/3, 91.
5. *BC* 9.41. See the whole statement in the Confession of 1967 on "Revelation and Religion," 9.41–42. See also *A Declaration of Faith* 7.4, "The church encounters other faiths."

6. Calvin, *Institutes* IV.20.3, 9.
7. Calvin, *Institutes* II.2, 15, 16.
8. The Declaration of Faith of the Congregational Church in England and Wales (III.6) says of the Holy Spirit: "Nor is his gracious presence confined to the Church. Even where his relation to Christ is not understood, where his presence is undiscerned, where his every existence is denied, there too God works perpetually in the Holy Spirit to enlarge the possibilities of human life and to turn men from self-centered isolation toward himself, their living God."
9. Newbigin, *The gospel in a Pluralistic Society,* 175.
10. Pinnock, *A Wideness in God's Mercy,* 138ff. (emphasis mine).
11. See Calvin, *Institutes* III.7.6: "We are not to consider what men merit of themselves but to look upon the image of God in all men, to which we owe all honor and love. . . . Therefore, whatever man you meet who needs your aid, you have no reason to refuse to help him. Say, 'He is a stranger'; but the Lord has given him a mark that ought to be familiar to you, by virtue of the fact that he forbids you to despise your own flesh. . . . Say, 'He is contemptible and worthless'; but the Lord shows him to be one to whom he has deigned to give the beauty of his image. Say that you owe him nothing for any service of his; but God, as it were, has put him in his own place in order that you may recognize toward him the many and great benefits with which God has bound you to himself. Say that he does not deserve even your least effort for his sake; but the image of God, which recommends him to you, is worthy of giving yourself and all your possessions. Now if he has not only deserved no good at your hand, but has also provoked you by unjust acts and curses, not even this is just reason why you should cease to embrace him in love and to perform the duties of love in his behalf. . . ."
12. Pinnock, *A Wideness in God's Mercy,* 141. Warren's statement is quoted from the foreword to John V. Taylor, *The Primal Vision: Christians Amid African Religions* (Philadelphia: Fortress Press, 1963), 10f.
13. Newbigen, *The gospel in a Pluralistic Society,* 166.
14. Paul Lehmann, *Ethics in a Christian Context* (New York: Harper & Row, 1963), 85.
15. Pinnock, *A Wideness in God's Mercy,* 153.

Notes for Chapter 6

1. In the following discussion, I have been helped especially by Jürgen Moltmann, *The Spirit of Life* (Minneapolis: Fortress Press, 1992); and by Hendrikus Berkhof, *The Doctrine of the Holy Spirit* (Richmond: John Knox Press, 1967). Moltmann draws heavily on Berkhof's earlier work, which came from his Warfield Lectures in 1964.

2. See Berkhof, *The Doctrine of the Holy Spirit,* 94ff.

3. Calvin, *Institutes* II.2.15–16 (emphasis added).

4. Berkhof, *The Doctrine of the Holy Spirit,* 21ff.

5. I have previously discussed these points in more detail in the revised edition of *Christian Doctrine* (Louisville, Ky.: Westminster John Knox Press, 1994), 298ff.

6. According to the Declaration of Faith, 6.3, "We must test any word that comes to us from church, world, or inner experience by the Word of God in Scripture."

7. Calvin, *Institutes* III.7.1, 5.

8. Contemporary Reformed confessions of faith, in contrast to earlier ones, often speak of the work of the Holy Spirit in the world outside the "Christian sphere." "In the Holy Spirit God is present and works in the midst of the world. He cares for, frees and governs this world in the framework of the realization of the Kingdom of God" (Church of Toraja, V.2). See also Declaration of Faith, Congregational Church in England and Wales, III.6, quoted in chap. 5, n.8, above.

9. The heading for this section of our discussion comes from Dietrich Bonhoeffer, *Life Together* (New York: Harper & Row, 1954).

10. In contrast to earlier Reformed confessions of faith, contemporary ones typically emphasize the fact that the gifts of the Spirit are given to individual Christians and the church for the sake of the church's mission to the world and service of the kingdom of God in the world. So, for instance, the Confession of 1967: "God the Holy Spirit fulfills the work of reconciliation in man. . . . [He] creates and renews the church as the community in which men are reconciled to God and to one another. . . . He gives them power to become representatives of Jesus Christ and his gospel of reconciliation to all men" (*BC,* 9.20).

11. See Moltmann, *The Spirit of Life,* 217ff.